THE MAGIC OF ASIA

THE MAGIC OF ASIA

Exotic and aromatic dishes from the East

KIM CHUNG LEE

LORENZ BOOKS

First published in 2000 by Lorenz Books

© 2000 Anness Publishing Limited

Lorenz Books is an imprint of
Anness Publishing Inc.
27 West 20th Street
New York, NY 10011; (800) 354-9657

ISBN 0 7548 0239 6

Publisher Joanna Lorenz
Project Editor Debra Mayhew
Designed by Wilson Harvey; *Food illustrations* Madeleine David, Anna Koska
Jacket photography Sam Stowell; *Jacket stylist* Antonia Gaunt; *Food for jacket* Eliza Baird

Recipes by Alex Barker, Kit Chan, Kim Chung Lee, Roz Denny, Rafi Fernandez, Christine France, Sarah Gates,
Shirley Gill, Shehzad Husain, Sallie Morris, Liz Trigg, Deh-Ta Tsuing, Steven Wheeler.
Food photography Karl Adamson, Edward Allwright, David Armstrong, Steve Baxter, James Duncan, Michelle Garrett, Amanda Heywood,
Michael Michaels, Juliet Piddington.
Food for photography Kit Chan, Carole Handslip, Shezad Husain, Wendy Lee, Jane Stevenson, Carol Tennant, Steven Wheeler, Elizabeth Wolf-Cohen.
Stylists Madelaine Brehaut, Michelle Garrett, Maria Kelly, Blake Minton, Marion Price, Kirsty Rawlings.

Previously published as separate volumes in the *Classic* series.

Printed and bound in Singapore

1 3 5 7 9 10 8 6 4 2

CONTENTS

INTRODUCTION

As the world's largest continent and home to some of the greatest ancient civilizations, it is not surprising that Asia has also developed a noble cuisine to match. Geography, climate, culture and religion have all played their parts in shaping the unique cuisine of Pakistan, India, Thailand, Vietnam, Malaysia, Indonesia, China and Japan. Traders, colonists and tourists later helped to cross-fertilize the techniques and ingredients of these countries, blurring their origins and letting each nation to put their own culinary stamp on them.

While Asian cuisine reflects these differences, it also shares many common features. Throughout Asia, cooking is a source of personal pride and eating is a pleasurable, social occasion. Asian cooks strive for a harmonious balance of flavors, textures, colors and aromas. Using only the freshest and quality ingredients, they prepare them with care to ensure that each flavor is brought out in the dish. A meal includes many dishes, which are all placed on the table at one time and eaten in no particular order. There will always be rice or noodle dishes, a soup, a curry, a steamed or fried dish, a salad and a dipping sauce or relishes.

This book offers an introduction to this diverse and delicious cuisine. Clear, step-by-step instructions make it simple to prepare these dishes at home. In no time you will create curries, make sushi, cook perfect basmati rice, prepare miso soup and assemble spring rolls. With a glossary of all the unusual ingredients and methods, cooks who are new to Asian cooking will find these recipes easy to follow and guaranteed to produce successful dishes. "Priti bhoja," as they say in India, "ching ching", as they say in China, or closer to home, just "enjoy!"

LEFT: (clockwise from top left) fenugreek, curry leaves, and cilantro leaves.

GUIDE TO INGREDIENTS

Adzuki beans
Small, red beans that are related to the soybean, used in rice dishes or sweetened and used in desserts; also available in glacé form (ama-natto) or in a paste (neri-an).

Special ingredients give Asian dishes their distinctive tastes: (CLOCKWISE FROM TOP LEFT) Nari, which is also known as pickled ginger; the Chinese spice, star anise; sesame seeds, which can also be toasted.

Almonds
Blanched almonds are available whole, sliced and ground and impart a sumptuous richness to curries. They are considered a great delicacy in India, where they are extremely expensive.

Bamboo shoots
The edible young shoots of the bamboo plant. Pale to bright yellow when bought fresh. Fresh bamboo shoots need some preparation and take quite a long time to cook. When buying canned shoots, look out for the whole ones as they seem to be better quality than the ready-sliced canned bamboo shoots.

Banana leaves
Glossy, dark green leaves of the banana tree are used to line steamers or wrap foods such as chicken or fish prior to broiling or baking. They have a slight flavor of fine tea.

Basil
A pungent herb that is used widely in Mediterranean and Southeast Asian cooking. Three varieties are used in Thai cooking: *bai mangluk* (hairy basil), *bai horapa* (sweet basil) and *bai grapao* (holy basil). Of these, *bai horapa* is the most popular. It has small, dark leaves with reddish-purple stems and flowers. Its flavor is reminiscent of aniseed and somewhat stronger than that of the western sweet basil.

Basmati rice
Light and fragrant rice grown in the foothills of the Himalayan mountains. Basmati makes the perfect base for pilaf dishes.

Bay leaves
The large dried leaves of the bay laurel tree are one of the oldest herbs used in cooking.

Bean curd
Known also as tofu or dofu, this is a flavorless curd made from soybeans that is rich in vitamins and minerals. It is available fresh, long-life or dried. It is a common ingredient in Chinese dishes and is a good source of protein for vegetarians.

Bean sauce
Made from salted and fermented soybeans, this sauce is a popular flavouring agent in Asian dishes. It is also called yellow bean sauce.

Bean sprouts
Sprouted from mung beans, they are used in salads and in stir-fried dishes, either raw or cooked. Look for crisp, firm sprouts with little scent.

Pungent ingredients add aromatic interest to Asian dishes: (CLOCKWISE FROM TOP LEFT) red and green chiles; bay leaves; garlic.

Bok choy
A Chinese cabbage that has thick white stalks and dark green leaves.

Bonito
The Pacific bonito is a small tuna that is commonly used in Japanese cooking. It is the strongest flavored of the tuna and is used dried in thin flakes known as katsuo-bushi. The flakes are used for seasoning.

Burdock
A long, thin root vegetable which is also known as gobo. It may be soaked to remove any bitterness and eaten raw or cooked.

Cardamom pods
A spice native to India, where its value is considered second only to that of saffron.

Cashews
These full-flavored nuts are a popular ingredient in many Asian cuisines.

Chana dhal
A round split yellow lentil, similar in appearance to the smaller moong dhal and the larger yellow split pea, which can be used as a substitute. It is used as a binding agent in some dishes and is widely available at Asian stores.

Chapati flour
A type of whole-wheat flour used to make chapatis and other breads.

Chickpeas
A nutty tasting pulse that is widely used in Indian vegetarian dishes.

Chiles
Hot peppers in many varieties. Their fire comes from the seeds, which can be removed for a milder flavor. Dried chile peppers can be used whole or coarsely crushed.

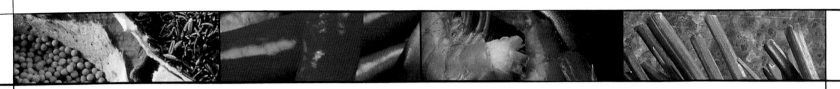

Chili powder
Also known as cayenne pepper, this is a fiery ground spice which should be used with caution.

Cinnamon
One of the earliest known spices with an aromatic and sweet flavor. It is sold ready-ground or as sticks.

Cloves
The dried flower bud of a tropical

(LEFT): Daikon is a long white radish with a peppery flavor. (RIGHT): Tiny pea eggplant add flavor to Thai dishes.

tree, used whole or ground as a spice.

Coconut
Used to flavor both sweet and savory dishes and can be substituted with any shredded coconut.

Coconut milk
The unsweetened liquid made from grated coconut flesh and water, which is an essential ingredient of many Thai dishes. It comes in cans, compressed blocks or in powdered form.

Coriander
Also known as cilantro or Chinese parsley. This is a beautifully fragrant herb from which the leaves, seeds and roots are used in Chinese, Indian and Thai cuisine. It is also used sprinkled on dishes as an attractive garnish.

Coriander Seeds
An aromatic spice with a pungent and slightly lemony flavor. The seeds are used either coarsely ground or in powdered form, in meat, poultry and fish dishes. Ground coriander is an important part of any curry powder.

Cumin
White cumin seeds are oval, ridged and greenish-brown in color. They have a strong aroma and flavor and can be used whole or ground. Ready-ground cumin powder is widely available. Black cumin seeds are dark and aromatic and are used to flavor curries and rice.

Curry leaves
Similar in appearance to bay leaves but with a very different flavor, they are available dried, and sometimes fresh, at Asian stores. Fresh leaves freeze well.

Curry paste
Traditionally made by pounding fresh herbs and spices together in a mortar. This is a time-consuming process but the finished product tastes delicious and keeps well. Ready-made pastes

are good, convenient alternatives.

Daikon
A long white radish that is also called mooli. About the size of a parsnip, daikon has a crunchy texture and peppery flavor similar to red radishes but milder. It may be cooked or served raw in salads.

Dashi
A stock used in Japanese cookery and usually made from kombu seaweed.

Dried mushrooms
These include a variety of mushrooms: black mushrooms, cloud ears and wood ears, which turn meaty and

Asian dishes feature a large variety of noodles: (FROM LEFT TO RIGHT) cellophane noodles; Somen noodles; egg noodles.

succulent when soaked in water.

Egg noodles
Made from wheat flour, egg and water. The dough is flattened and shredded to the required shape and thickness.

Eggplant
A vegetable fruit with a mildly sweet

flavor. Many varieties of eggplant are used in Thai cooking, from the tiny pea eggplant to white, green or yellow eggplant. When these types are unavailable, use the purple variety.

Enoki mushrooms
Long stems and tiny white caps. They are crisp with a delicate flavor.

Fennel seeds
Very similar in appearance to cumin seeds, with a very sweet taste. These are used to flavor certain curries or can also be chewed as a mouth-freshener after a spicy meal.

Fenugreek
This is available fresh or as seeds. The fresh variety is sold in bunches and has very small leaves which are used to flavor meat and vegetarian dishes. The stalks must be discarded or they will make the food bitter. The seeds are very pungent and slightly bitter.

Fish sauce
The most commonly used flavoring in Thai food, along the lines of soy sauce for Chinese food. It is made from salted anchovies and has a strong salty flavor.

Five-spice powder
A mixture of aniseed, cinnamon, fennel seed, cloves and Szechuan pepper used in Chinese cooking.

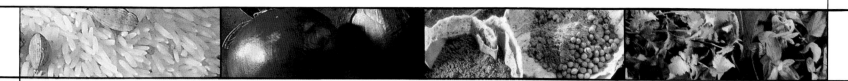

Galangal

A member of the ginger family that looks similar to fresh ginger root, but with a more translucent skin and a pinkish tinge. It has a wonderful sharp, lemony taste and is prepared in a similar way to ginger root. Best used fresh, it is also available dried or powdered.

(LEFT) Onion seeds are widely used in pickles. (RIGHT) Cloves can be used whole to impart flavor, and then removed, or ground as a spice.

Garam masala

A mixture of Indian spices that can be made from freshly ground spices at home or bought ready-made. A typical mixture might include black cumin seeds, peppercorns, cloves, cinnamon and black cardamom pods.

Garlic

A very important ingredient in Asian cooking. Look out for fresh shiny heads. Avoid soft, dusty or moldy cloves. Jars of pickled garlic can be bought at Asian stores.

Ginger root

A root of Chinese and Indian origin. It should either be peeled and chopped or crushed before cooking. Not as popular as galangal in Thai cooking, but a useful alternative. Dried ginger makes a good standby if fresh is not available.

Hijiki

Dried seaweed that is soaked and used in soups and salads.

Hoisin sauce

Also known as barbecue sauce, it is made from soybeans and has a dark reddish-brown color with a hot and sweet flavor.

Kaffir lime

Similar to the common lime but with a bumpy skin. The zest is often used and the dark, glossy, green leaves from the tree give a pungent lemony-lime flavor to soups, curries and other dishes. Bought fresh at Asian stores, the leaves keep well and can also be frozen. Dried Kaffir limes are also available.

Katakuri–ko

Potato starch or flour; cornstarch can be used as an alternative. Available at Asian shops.

Kelp

Kelp seaweed is used to flavor stock and is also served as a vegetable

Kombu

Dried kombu is a dark gray-brown color with a pale powdery covering.

Konnyaku

A cake made from flour produced from a root vegetable called devil's tongue. Tear it into pieces before cooking so that it absorbs more flavor. Black and white varieties are both available.

Lemongrass

An aromatic tropical grass that is also known as citronella. Lemongrass characterizes Thai and Vietnamese cuisine. It has a long, pale green stalk and a bulbous end—similar to a scallion. Only the bottom portion

(LEFT) Indian cooking uses bright yellow turmeric to add color to dishes. (RIGHT) Dried red chiles are extremely hot and can be used whole or crushed.

is used, and it should be crushed lightly before chopping to release more flavor.

Lengkuas

A member of the ginger family, available either in fresh, dried or powdered form.

Masoor dhal

Red split lentils that turn pale yellow when cooked.

Mirin

A sweet version of cooking sake, this has a delicate flavor and is usually added in the final stages of cooking.

Miso

A fermented paste of soybeans, which forms the key ingredient of miso soup and is also used as a seasoning. There are various types of miso, which may be based on barley, wheat or soybean starter mold. The lightest flavor is from white miso; red miso is saltier while dark brown miso has a stronger flavor.

Moong dhal

Teardrop-shaped split yellow lentils that are similar to, though smaller than, chana dhal.

Mustard seeds

Round in shape and sharp in flavor, black mustard seeds are used for flavoring curries and pickles.

Nari

Pale pink ginger pickles that are served with sushi or sashimi, to refresh the palate between bites.

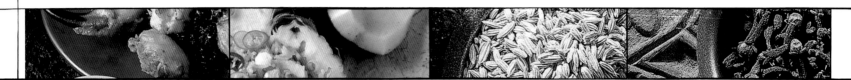

Noodles

An important ingredient in Chinese, Japanese, Thai and other Asian dishes. Cellophane noodles are made from ground mung beans and are commonly called bean thread, glass or transparent noodles. Dried noodles must be soaked in hot water before using. Egg noodles are made from wheat flour, egg and water. Rice noodles are made from ground rice and water and range in thickness from very thin to wide ribbons and sheets. Rinse rice noodles in warm water and drain well before use. Rice vermicelli is a thin, brittle noodle that looks like white hair and is sold in large bundles. They cook almost instantly in hot liquid, provided the noodles are first soaked in warm water. Soba noodles are made from a mixture of buckwheat and wheat flour. They are traditionally cooked in simmering water, then drained and served hot in winter or cold in summer with a dipping sauce. Somen noodles are delicate, thin white Japanese noodles made from wheat flour, tied in bundles and held together with a paper band. Udon noodles are made from wheat flour and water. They are usually round, but can also be flat and are available fresh, precooked or dried at Asian stores.

Nori

Dried seaweed is sold in paper-thin sheets that are dark green to black in color and almost transparent in places. It is toasted and then used as a wrapping for sushi.

Onion seeds

Black, triangular seeds that are widely used in pickles and to flavor vegetable curries.

Oyster sauce

A thickish, slightly sweet and salty brown-colored sauce made from oyster extract, soy sauce, sugar and vinegar. It is used to flavor meat, fish and vegetable dishes. A vegetarian version made from a mushroom base is also available.

Palm sugar

Strongly flavored, hard brown sugar made from the sap of the coconut palm tree. Dark brown sugar will

Chapatis, and other Indian breads, are made from a special whole-wheat flour.

substitute if you cannot find it at Asian stores.

Peppercorns

One of the spices used to flavor curries. Good used freshly ground or crushed in recipes where black pepper is called for.

Pickles

Pickled vegetables (tsukemono) are often served with rice dishes. Fresh ginger root is also pickled in various strengths of flavor.

Pomegranate seeds

These can be extracted from fresh pomegranates or bought in jars at

Basmati rice is traditionally grown in the foothills of the Himalayan mountains. It is delicious flavored with cardamom pods.

Asian stores and give a delicious tangy flavor.

Red bean paste

Made from red kidney beans and sugar and used as a dip or spread on pancakes served with Peking Duck.

Rice vinegar

A pale vinegar that has a distinctive, delicate flavor.

Rice wine

Made from fermented glutinous, sticky rice, this golden wine is used for both drinking and cooking.

Saffron

The world's most expensive spice is the dried stigmas of the saffron crocus, which is native to Asia Minor. To produce 1 pound of saffron requires 60,000 stigmas, but only a small amount of saffron is needed to flavor and color a dish. It is sold in threads and in powder form.

Sake

Japanese rice wine. It is not necessary to use expensive sake for cooking. Sake is drunk hot or chilled.

Sashimi

Slices of raw fish sushi used in Japanese cuisine.

Sesame oil

A nutty-flavored oil extracted from toasted sesame seeds.

Sesame seeds

Black or white, these are available roasted or plain. Toast the plain seeds before using.

Seven-flavor spice or pepper

A chili-based spice made of hemp, poppy, rape and sesame seeds, tangerine peel and anise-pepper

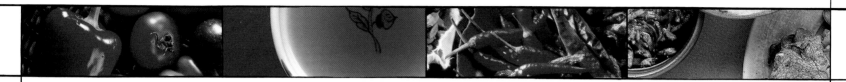

leaves. It is used as a seasoning or condiment for noodle dishes and is available at Japanese food shops. Also known as sci-chimi.

Shallots
Thai shallots have a lovely pinkish-purple color and are used widely in Thai cuisine instead of onions.

Shiitake mushrooms
The most popular mushroom in Japan, these have a good flavor, especially if dried. Soaking water from dried shiitake makes a good stock.

Shiratama-ko
Rice flour made from glutinous short-grain rice with a high starch content.

Shiso leaves
A Japanese herb similar to basil.

Soy sauce
An essential ingredient in Asian cooking, particularly stir-fries and noodle dishes, soy sauce is made from fermented soybeans and ranges in color from pale to dark, the lighter having more flavor than the sweeter dark variety.

Star anise
A spice used in Chinese dishes. It comes in the form of a dried, star-shaped seed pod that is usually added to braised and simmered dishes to give them an aniseed-like flavor.

Sushi
Different varieties of fresh uncooked fish pressed on rice.

Sushi vinegar
A seasoned and sweetened vinegar product for sushi.

Enoki mushrooms are delicious eaten raw.

Szechuan peppercorns
Used in Chinese dishes, these are reddish-brown in color, and have a spicier, although less hot flavor than black peppercorns.

Tamarind
An acidic tropical fruit that resembles a bean pod. It is usually sold dried or pulped. To make tamarind juice, take 1 ounce of tamarind or about 2 stock cube-size pieces and let soak in ²/₃ cup of warm water for about 10 minutes. Squeeze out as much tamarind juice as possible by pressing all the liquid through a sieve.

Terasi
Shrimp paste made from fermented shrimp and salt. Sold in blocks.

Tofu
Also known as bean curd or dofu, this is a soybean product valued for its high protein content. It is useful in a vegetarian diet; it is also a good source of calcium and iron. There are several types, including soft or firm tofu, silken tofu, broiled tofu and dried tofu. Deep-fried tofu is sold ready-made at Japanese stores.

Toor dhal
A shiny split yellow lentil, toor dhal is similar in size to chana dhal.

Turmeric
A bright yellow, bitter-tasting spice sold ground. It is used mainly for color rather than flavor.

Thick, glossy, dark green banana leaves are widely used to line steamers or to wrap food prior to broiling or baking.

Umeboshi
Small red pickled plums with a sharp and salty taste. They are considered a preservative and used to fill rice balls.

Urid dhal
Also known as black gram, this lentil is similar in size to moong dhal and is available either with the blackish hull retained or removed.

Vinegar
Thais use a mild, plain white vinegar. The Japanese use rice vinegar, a light and mild vinegar.

Wakame
Vacuum-packed or dried seaweed, for soups and salads.

Wasasbi
Green horseradish that tastes extremely hot. Available as a paste or a powder, to which water is added.

Wonton wrappers
Small square sheets rolled from egg-noodle dough, these are available in packages from Chinese food markets.

Yellow bean sauce
This is made from salted, fermented soybeans and added to flavor many savory Asian dishes.

BASIC RECIPES

There are a few spice mixtures and stocks that form the basis of Asian cooking. They are not difficult or time-consuming to make and can be stored for weeks and used when needed. Ready-made versions are readily available, but it is worth spending the time needed to produce a fresh, authentic version.

HOMEMADE GARAM MASALA

Garam masala is a mixture of spices that is used to flavor many Indian dishes. It can be made from freshly ground spices at home or bought ready-made. A typical mixture might include cumin seeds, peppercorns, cloves, cinnamon, bay leaves and nutmeg. In some versions, black cardamom pods and fenugreek seeds are added.

INGREDIENTS
3-inch piece cinnamon stick
2 bay leaves
1 teaspoon black cumin seeds
1 teaspoon whole cloves
1 teaspoon black peppercorns
¼ nutmeg, grated

1 Break the cinnamon sticks into pieces. Crumble the bay leaves.

2 Heat a small frying pan over medium heat, then add the bay leaves and all the spices except the nutmeg.

3 Dry-fry until the spices turn a shade darker and emit a roasted aroma, stirring or shaking the pan frequently to prevent burning.

4 Let cool. Place all the ingredients in a spice mill or electric coffee grinder and grind into a fine powder. Store in a small jar with a tight-fitting lid for up to 2 months.

THAI RED CURRY PASTE

All curry making begins with the curry paste. Although traditionally made with a mortar and pestle, a blender or food processor produces a delicious paste in seconds.

INGREDIENTS
1-inch piece fresh ginger
    root, chopped
4 shallots, finely sliced
4-6 garlic cloves, chopped
4 lemongrass stalks, peeled
    and chopped
4 fresh red chiles, seeded
    and chopped
4 teaspoons coriander seeds
2 teaspoons cumin seeds
2 teaspoons hot paprika
¼ teaspoon ground turmeric
½ teaspoon salt
grated zest and juice of 2 limes
1 tablespoon vegetable oil

1 Heat a small frying pan over medium heat and add the coriander and cumin seeds. Toss them in the pan until the spices turn a shade darker and emit a roasted aroma. Let cool.

2 Peel and chop the ginger, shallots and garlic. Peel and finely chop the lemongrass. Peel and roughly chop the chiles as directed on the next page.

3 Place all the ingredients in a blender or food processor and process together to form a smooth paste.

4 Store in a screw-top jar for up to 1 month in the refrigerator and use as needed.

BASIC TECHNIQUES

For the ingredients to cook quickly and still absorb the taste of the oil and flavoring, they should be cut into small uniform pieces with as many cut surfaces as possible exposed to the heat. Careful cutting also enhances the visual appeal of a dish—a factor that is very important in Asian cuisines.

CHOPPING CHILES

The fire in chiles comes from the seeds, so discard them for a milder flavor. Chiles contain an oil that can irritate the skin and eyes. Wash hands thoroughly and avoid touching the face or eyes after cutting chiles, or wear rubber gloves.

1 Slice the chiles, and then remove the seeds. It is advisable to wear rubber gloves to protect your skin.

2 Finely chop the chiles and use as required.

PEELING AND CHOPPING LEMONGRASS

Aromatic lemongrass can be bought at Asian food stores and some larger supermarkets.

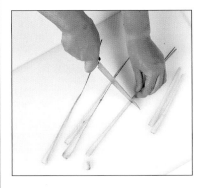 

1 Cut off and discard the dry leafy tops, leaving about 6-inch of stalk. Peel off any tough outer layers from the lemongrass.

2 Lay the lemongrass on a board. Set a cleaver or chef's knife on top and strike it firmly with your fist; this helps to extract maximum flavor. Cut across the lemongrass to make thin slices, then continue chopping until fine.

CHOPPING MEAT FOR STIR-FRYING

The speed of this method of cooking requires meat to be cut as thinly as possible. Always use a sharp bladed knife.

1 Beef is always cut across the grain otherwise it will become tough; pork, lamb and chicken can be cut either along or across the grain.

2 Placing the meat in the freezer for about 1 hour beforehand makes it easier to cut paper-thin slices.

CUTTING JULIENNE STRIPS

After cooking, julienne strips of vegetables can be tied in individual bundles with a chive and used as an appealing and edible garnish.

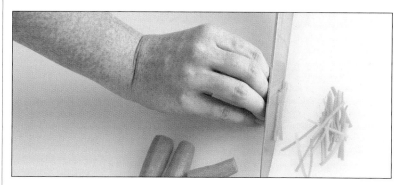

1 Peel the vegetable and use a large knife to cut it into 2-inch lengths. Cut a thin sliver from one side of the first piece so that it will sit flat on the board.

2 Cut each strip, lengthwise, into thin wedges.

3 Stack the slices and then cut through them to make fine strips (*above*).

APPETIZERS

Appetizers are a Western phenomenon. While Western cultures begin their meals with a soup or savory dish, Asian countries serve one large course, combining soups, rice, noodles, vegetables, protein and pulses. The importance here is to harmoniously balance flavors, colors, cooking methods and ingredients and then enjoy the results in any order.

For Western consumers, the typical Asian dishes offer many delicious titbits that are perfect for appetizers. For example, delicate quail's eggs are marbled in lapsang souchong tea for a fragrant and attractive appetizer from China. For a more substantial start, Pan-steamed Mussels with Thai Herbs takes an already delicious seafood dish and brings it alive with the tangy flavor of lemongrass and the spice of red chiles.

Familiar soups based on chicken or vegetables also get a twist with the addition of flavorful Asian ingredients including cilantro, ginger root, kaffir lime leaves, soy sauce, dashi and tamarind.

CHICKEN AND ALMOND SOUP

T his soup makes an excellent appetizer and, served with naan, will also make a satisfying lunch or supper dish.

INGREDIENTS
6 tablespoons unsalted butter
1 leek, chopped
½ teaspoon sliced fresh ginger root
1 cup ground almonds
1 teaspoon salt
½ teaspoon crushed black peppercorns
1 fresh green chile, chopped
4 ounces chicken, skinned, boned and cubed
1 carrot, sliced
½ cup frozen peas
1 tablespoon chopped cilantro
scant 2 cups water
1 cup light cream
4 cilantro sprigs, to garnish

SERVES 4

1 Melt the butter in a large karahi or deep round frying pan and sauté the leek with the ginger until soft.

2 Lower the heat and add the ground almonds, salt, peppercorns, chile, chicken, carrot and peas. Fry for about 10 minutes or until the chicken is completely cooked, stirring constantly. Add the chopped cilantro.

3 Remove the pan from heat and let cool slightly. Transfer the mixture to a food processor or blender and process for about 1½ minutes. Pour in the water and blend for another 30 seconds.

4 Pour the puréed mixture back into the karahi or frying pan and bring slowly to a boil, stirring occasionally. Once the soup has boiled, lower the heat and gradually stir in the cream. Cook the soup, without bringing to a boil, for another 2 minutes, stirring occasionally, until the cream is just heated through.

5 To serve, transfer the soup to warmed individual bowls, garnish each one with a cilantro sprig and serve immediately.

SPICY CHICKEN AND MUSHROOM SOUP

T he combination of hot spices and cream makes this soup a perfect warming dish for a winter's night.

INGREDIENTS
8 ounces chicken, skinned and boned
6 tablespoons unsalted butter
½ garlic clove, crushed
1 teaspoon garam masala
1 teaspoon crushed black peppercorns
1 teaspoon salt
¼ teaspoon ground nutmeg
1 leek, sliced
1 cup mushrooms, sliced
⅓ cup corn
1¼ cups water
1 cup light cream
1 tablespoon chopped cilantro
1 teaspoon crushed dried red chiles
(optional), to garnish

SERVES 4

1 Using a sharp knife, cut the chicken pieces into very fine strips. Melt the butter in a saucepan and add the garlic and garam masala. Lower the heat and add the peppercorns, salt and nutmeg. Finally, add the strips of chicken, sliced leek, mushrooms and corn and cook for 5–7 minutes or until the chicken is cooked through, stirring constantly.

2 Remove the saucepan from heat and let the chicken mixture cool slightly. Transfer three-quarters of the mixture to a food processor or blender. Add the water and process for about 1 minute, until smooth.

3 Stir the purée back into the saucepan with the rest of the mixture and bring to a boil over medium heat. Lower the heat and stir in the cream.

4 Add the cilantro, then taste for seasoning. Serve hot, garnished with the crushed red chiles, if using.

SHRIMP WITH POMEGRANATE SEEDS

GRILLED SHRIMP

Jumbo shrimp are the best choice for this dish. It makes an great appetizer for a dinner party, and is delicious served with a mixed salad.

INGREDIENTS

1 teaspoon crushed garlic
1 teaspoon sliced fresh ginger root
1 teaspoon coarsely ground pomegranate seeds
1 teaspoon ground cilantro
1 teaspoon salt
1 teaspoon chili powder
2 tablespoons tomato paste
¼ cup water
3 tablespoons chopped cilantro
2 tablespoons corn oil
12 large cooked shrimp
1 onion, sliced into rings

SERVES 4–6

1 Put the garlic, ginger, pomegranate seeds, ground coriander, salt, chili powder, tomato paste, water and 2 tablespoons of the cilantro into a bowl. Pour in the oil and blend thoroughly.

2 Peel the shrimp. Using a sharp knife, make a small slit at the back of each shrimp, then gently open them out to make a butterfly shape.

3 Add the shrimp to the spice mixture, coating them well. Cover and let marinate for about 2 hours.

4 Cut four squares of aluminum foil, each about 8 × 8 inches. Preheat the oven to 450°F. Place three shrimp and a few onion rings on each square of foil, garnishing them with a little cilantro, and fold up into little packages. Bake the shrimp for 12–15 minutes and open up the foil packages to serve.

OPPOSITE: A mixed salad (TOP) is delicious with Shrimp with Pomegranate Seeds (CENTER) and Grilled Shrimp (BOTTOM)

Shrimp are delicious broiled, especially when they are flavored with spices.

INGREDIENTS

¼ cup lemon juice
1 teaspoon salt
1 teaspoon chili powder
1 garlic clove, crushed
1½ teaspoons light brown sugar
3 tablespoons corn oil
2 tablespoons chopped cilantro
18 large peeled, cooked shrimp
1 fresh green chile, sliced
1 tomato, sliced
1 small onion, cut into rings
lemon wedges, to garnish

SERVES 4–6

1 Combine the lemon juice, salt, chili powder, garlic, sugar, corn oil and cilantro in a bowl. Add the shrimp, coating them well. Cover and let marinate for about 1 hour.

2 Place the green chile, tomato slices and onion rings in a flameproof dish. Add the shrimp mixture and cook under a preheated very hot broiler for 10–15 minutes, basting several times. Serve immediately, garnished with the lemon wedges.

HOT-AND-SOUR SHRIMP SOUP WITH LEMONGRASS

his is a classic seafood soup—*Tom Yam Goong*—and is probably the most popular of Thai soups.

INGREDIENTS

1 pound jumbo shrimp (raw or cooked)
4 cups chicken stock or water
3 lemongrass stalks
10 kaffir lime leaves, torn in half
8-ounce can straw mushrooms, drained
3 tablespoons fish sauce
¼ cup lime juice
2 tablespoons chopped scallions
1 tablespoon cilantro leaves
4 red chiles, seeded and chopped

SERVES 4–6

1 Shell and devein the shrimp and set aside. Rinse the shrimp shells, place in a large saucepan with the stock or water and bring to a boil.

2 Bruise the lemongrass stalks with the blunt edge of a chopping knife and add them to the stock together with half of the lime leaves. Simmer gently for 5–6 minutes, until the stalks change color and the stock is fragrant.

3 Strain the stock, return to the saucepan and reheat. Add the mushrooms and shrimp, then cook for a few minutes or until the shrimp turn pink if raw.

4 Stir in the fish sauce, lime juice, scallions, cilantro, chiles and the rest of the lime leaves. Taste; adjust the flavors. It should be sour, salty, spicy and hot.

SPINACH AND TOFU SOUP

An extremely delicate and mild-flavored soup that can be used to counterbalance the heat from a hot Thai curry.

INGREDIENTS
2 tablespoons dried shrimp
4 cups chicken stock
8 ounces fresh tofu, drained and cut into
¾-inch cubes
2 tablespoons fish sauce
12 ounces fresh spinach leaves,
thoroughly washed
freshly ground black pepper
2 scallions, finely sliced, to garnish

SERVES 4–6

3 Tear the spinach leaves into bite-size pieces and add to the soup. Cook for another 1–2 minutes.

4 Remove the soup from heat, ladle into bowls and sprinkle on the finely sliced scallions, to garnish.

1 Rinse and drain the dried shrimp. Combine the shrimp with the chicken stock in a saucepan and bring to a boil.

2 Add the tofu and simmer for about 5 minutes. Season with fish sauce and black pepper to taste.

THAI CHICKEN SOUP

A spicy light soup sweetened with coconut and crunchy peanut butter for added bite.

INGREDIENTS

1 tablespoon vegetable oil
1 garlic clove, finely chopped
6 ounces boned chicken breasts, skinned and chopped
½ teaspoon ground turmeric
¼ teaspoon hot chili powder
3 ounces coconut milk
3¾ cups hot chicken stock
dash of lemon juice
2 tablespoons crunchy peanut butter
1 cup thread egg noodles, broken into small pieces
1 tablespoon scallions, finely chopped
1 tablespoon chopped cilantro
salt and freshly ground black pepper
2 tablespoons dry, shredded coconut and ½ fresh red chile, seeded and finely chopped, to garnish

SERVES 4

1 Heat the oil in a large pan and fry the garlic for 1 minute. Add the chicken and spices and stir-fry for another 3–4 minutes.

2 Add the coconut milk into the hot chicken stock and stir until dissolved. Pour this mixture onto the chicken and add the lemon juice, peanut butter and egg noodles.

3 Cover and simmer for about 15 minutes. Add the scallions and cilantro, then season well with salt and freshly ground black pepper and cook for another 5 minutes.

4 Meanwhile, place the coconut and chopped chile in a small frying pan and heat for about 3 minutes, stirring frequently, until the coconut is lightly browned.

5 Pour the soup into individual bowls and sprinkle with the fried coconut and chopped chile.

GOLDEN POUCHES

T hese crisp pouches from Thailand are delicious served as an appetizer or as finger food at a party.

INGREDIENTS
4 ounces ground pork
4 ounces crabmeat
2–3 wood ear mushrooms, soaked
and chopped
1 tablespoon chopped cilantro
1 teaspoon chopped garlic
2 tablespoons chopped scallions
1 egg
1 tablespoon fish sauce
1 teaspoon soy sauce
pinch of sugar
20 wonton wrappers
20 long chives, blanched (optional)
oil, for deep-frying
freshly ground black pepper
plum or sweet chili sauce, to serve

MAKES ABOUT 20

1 In a mixing bowl, combine the pork, crabmeat, wood ear mushrooms, cilantro, garlic, scallions and egg. Mix well and season with fish sauce, soy sauce, sugar and freshly ground black pepper.

2 Take a wonton wrapper and place it on a flat surface. Put a heaping teaspoonful of filling in the center of the wrapper, then pull up the edges of the pastry around the filling.

3 Pinch together to seal. If desired, you can go a step further and tie it with a long chive. Repeat with the remaining pork mixture and wonton wrappers.

4 Heat the oil in a wok or deep-fryer. Fry the wontons in batches until they are crisp and golden brown. Drain on paper towels and serve immediately with either a plum or sweet chili sauce.

STEAMED SEAFOOD PACKETS

Very neat and delicate, these steamed packets make an excellent appetizer or a light lunch. You can find glossy, green banana leaves at Asian food stores.

INGREDIENTS
8 ounces crabmeat
2 ounces shelled shrimp, chopped
6 water chestnuts, chopped
2 tablespoons chopped bamboo shoots
1 tablespoon chopped scallion
1 teaspoon chopped ginger root
1 tablespoon soy sauce
1 tablespoon fish sauce
12 sheets rice paper
banana leaves
oil, for brushing
2 scallions, shredded
2 red chiles, seeded and sliced,
and cilantro leaves, to garnish

SERVES 4

1 Combine the crabmeat, chopped shrimp, water chestnuts, bamboo shoots, chopped scallion and ginger in a bowl. Mix well, then add the soy sauce and fish sauce. Stir until blended.

2 Take a sheet of rice paper and dip it in warm water. Place it on a flat surface and set aside for a few seconds to soften.

3 Place a spoonful of the filling in the center of the sheet and fold into a square packet. Repeat with the rest of the rice paper and seafood mixture.

4 Use banana leaves to line a steamer, then brush them with oil. Place the packets, seam-side down, on the leaves and steam over high heat for 6–8 minutes or until the filling is cooked.

5 Transfer to a plate and serve, garnished with the shredded scallions, sliced chiles and cilantro.

COOK'S TIP
The seafood packets will spread out when steamed, so be sure to space them well apart to prevent them from sticking together.

PAN-STEAMED MUSSELS WITH THAI HERBS

nother simple dish to prepare. The lemongrass adds a refreshing tang to the mussels.

INGREDIENTS
2¼ pounds mussels, cleaned and beards removed
2 lemongrass stalks, finely chopped
4 shallots, chopped
4 kaffir lime leaves, roughly torn
2 red chiles, seeded and sliced
1 tablespoon fish sauce
2 tablespoons lime juice
2 scallions, chopped, and cilantro leaves, to garnish

SERVES 4–6

1 Place all the ingredients, except for the scallions and cilantro, in a large saucepan and stir thoroughly.

2 Cover and steam for 5–7 minutes, shaking the saucepan occasionally, until the mussels open. Discard any mussels that do not open.

3 Transfer the cooked mussels to a warmed serving dish.

4 Garnish the mussels with chopped scallions and cilantro leaves. Serve immediately.

FISH CAKES WITH CUCUMBER RELISH

 These wonderful small fish cakes are a familiar and popular appetizer, usually accompanied by Thai beer.

INGREDIENTS
11 ounces white fish fillet, such as cod, cut into chunks
2 tablespoons red curry paste
1 egg
2 tablespoons fish sauce
1 teaspoon granulated sugar
2 tablespoons cornstarch
3 kaffir lime leaves, shredded
1 tablespoon chopped cilantro
2 ounces green beans, finely sliced
oil, for frying
Chinese greens, to garnish

FOR THE CUCUMBER RELISH
¼ cup Thai coconut or rice vinegar
¼ cup water
2 ounces sugar
1 head of pickled garlic
1 cucumber, quartered and sliced
4 shallots, finely sliced
1 tablespoon finely chopped ginger root
2 red chiles, seeded and finely sliced

MAKES ABOUT 12

1 To make the cucumber relish, bring the vinegar, water and sugar to a boil. Stir until the sugar dissolves, then remove from heat and cool.

2 Combine the rest of the relish ingredients together in a bowl and pour in the vinegar mixture.

3 Combine the fish, curry paste and egg in a food processor and process well. Transfer the mixture to a bowl, add the rest of the ingredients, except for the oil and garnish, and mix well.

4 Mold and shape the mixture into cakes about 2 inches in diameter and ¼-inch thick.

5 Heat the oil in a wok or deep-fryer. Fry the fish cakes, a few at a time, for 4–5 minutes or until golden brown. Remove and drain on paper towels. Garnish with Chinese greens and serve with the cucumber relish.

HANOI BEEF AND NOODLE SOUP

his fragrant North Vietnamese soup, traditionally eaten for breakfast, makes a filling appetizer.

INGREDIENTS
1 onion
3–3¹/₂-pound beef shank with bones
1-inch piece fresh ginger root
1 star anise
1 bay leaf
2 whole cloves
¹/₂ teaspoon fennel seeds
1-inch piece of cassia bark or cinnamon stick
12¹/₂ cups water
fish sauce, to taste
juice of 1 lime
5 ounces beef fillet
1 pound fresh flat rice noodles

ACCOMPANIMENTS
1 small red onion, sliced into rings
4 ounces bean sprouts
2 red chiles, seeded and sliced
3 scallions, finely sliced
handful of cilantro leaves
lime wedges

SERVES 4–6

1 Cut the onion in half. Broil under high heat, cut-side up, until the exposed sides are caramelized and deep brown. Set aside.

2 Cut the bones from the meat, and chop into large chunks. Place the meat and the bones into a large saucepan or stock pot. Add the caramelized onion with the ginger, star anise, bay leaf, cloves, fennel seeds and cassia bark or cinnamon stick.

3 Add the water, bring to a boil, reduce the heat and simmer gently for 2–3 hours, occaionally skimming off the fat and white froth.

4 Using a slotted spoon, remove the meat from the stock; when cool enough to handle, cut into small pieces, discarding the bones. Strain the stock and return to the pan or stock pot together with the meat. Bring back to a boil and season with the fish sauce and lime juice.

5 Slice the beef very thinly and then chill until needed. Place the accompaniments in separate bowls so that everyone can help themselves.

6 Cook the noodles in a large saucepan of boiling water until just tender. Drain and divide among individual serving bowls. Arrange the thinly sliced beef on the noodles and pour the hot stock on top.

VIETNAMESE SPRING ROLLS

runchy spring rolls are the perfect appetizer, complemented here by *nuoc cham* sauce.

INGREDIENTS

6 dried Chinese mushrooms, soaked
8 ounces lean ground pork
4 ounces uncooked shrimp, peeled,
deveined and chopped
4 ounces white crabmeat, picked over
1 carrot, shredded
2 ounces cellophane noodles, soaked in
water, drained and cut into short lengths
4 scallions, finely sliced
2 garlic cloves, finely chopped
2 tablespoons fish sauce
juice of 1 lime
freshly ground black pepper
25 4-inch sheets of rice paper
oil, for deep -frying

FOR THE SAUCE

2 garlic cloves, finely chopped
2 tablespoons white wine vinegar
juice of 1 lime
2 tablespoons sugar
½ cup fish sauce
½ cup water
2 red chiles, seeded and chopped

MAKES 25

1 Drain the mushrooms. Remove and discard the stems and slice the caps into a bowl. Add the pork, shrimp, crabmeat, carrot, noodles, scallions and garlic.

2 Season with the fish sauce, lime juice and pepper. Set the mixture aside for 30 minutes to let the flavors blend.

3 Meanwhile make the *nuoc cham* sauce. Combine the garlic, vinegar, lime juice, sugar, fish sauce, water and chiles in a serving bowl, then cover and set aside.

4 Assemble the spring rolls. Brush a sheet of rice paper with warm water until pliable. Place 2 teaspoons of the filling near the edge of the sheet. Fold the sides over the filling, fold in the two ends, then roll up, sealing the ends with a little water.

5 Make more rolls until all the filling is used up. Then heat the oil for deep-frying to 350°F or until a cube of dry bread added to the oil browns in 30–45 seconds. Add the rolls, a few at a time, and fry until golden brown and crisp. Drain on paper towels. Serve hot, garnished with lettuce, cucumber, radish and cilantro, if desired. Pass the *nuoc cham* sauce in a separate bowl.

PORK SATE

O riginating in Indonesia, saté are skewers of meat marinated with spices and grilled quickly over charcoal. You can make them with chicken, beef or lamb.

INGREDIENTS
1 pound lean pork
1 teaspoon grated ginger root
1 lemongrass stalk, finely chopped
3 garlic cloves, finely chopped
1 tablespoon medium curry paste
1 teaspoon ground cumin
1 teaspoon ground turmeric
¼ cup coconut milk
2 tablespoons fish sauce
1 teaspoon sugar
20 wooden saté skewers
oil, for brushing
sprigs of mint, to garnish

FOR THE SATE SAUCE
1 cup coconut milk
2 tablespoons red curry paste
3 ounces crunchy peanut butter
½ cup chicken stock
3 tablespoons brown sugar
2 tablespoons tamarind juice
1 tablespoon fish sauce
½ teaspoon salt

MAKES ABOUT 20

1 Cut the pork thinly into 2-inch strips. Combine the ginger, lemongrass, garlic, medium curry paste, cumin, turmeric, coconut milk, fish sauce and sugar.

2 Pour over the pork and let marinate for about 2 hours.

3 Meanwhile, make the sauce. Heat the coconut milk over medium heat, then add the red curry paste, peanut butter, chicken stock and sugar.

4 Cook and stir until smooth, for 5–6 minutes. Add the tamarind juice, fish sauce and salt to taste.

5 Thread the meat onto skewers. Brush with oil and grill over charcoal or under a preheated broiler for 3–4 minutes on each side, turning occasionally, until cooked. Garnish with mint and serve with the saté sauce.

TAMARIND AND VEGETABLE SOUP

ayur Assam is a colorful and refreshing soup from Jakarta with more than a hint of sharpness.

INGREDIENTS
5 shallots or 1 medium red onion, sliced
3 garlic cloves, crushed
1-inch piece lengkuas, peeled and sliced
1–2 fresh red chiles, seeded and sliced
1 ounce raw peanuts
1/2-inch cube terasi, prepared
5 cups well-flavored stock
2–3 ounces salted peanuts, lightly crushed
1–2 tablespoons dark brown sugar
1 teaspoon tamarind pulp, soaked in 5 tablespoons warm water for 15 minutes
salt
1 fresh green chile, sliced, to garnish

FOR THE VEGETABLES
1 chayote, thinly peeled, seeds removed, flesh finely sliced
4 ounces green beans, trimmed and finely sliced
1/4 cup corn kernels
handful green leaves, such as watercress, arugula or Chinese greens, finely shredded

SERVES 4

1 Prepare the spice paste by grinding the shallots or onion, garlic, lengkuas, chiles, raw peanuts and terasi to a paste in a food processor or with a mortar and pestle.

2 Pour in some of the stock to moisten and then pour this mixture into a pan or wok, adding the rest of the stock. Cook for 15 minutes with the lightly crushed peanuts and sugar.

3 Strain the tamarind, discarding the seeds, and reserve the juice.

4 About 5 minutes before serving, add the chayote slices, beans and corn to the soup and cook fairly rapidly. At the last minute, add the green leaves and salt to taste.

5 Add the tamarind juice and taste for seasoning. Serve, garnished with slices of green chile.

GARLIC MUSHROOMS

T ofu is high in protein and very low in fat, so it is a very useful food to keep handy for quick and healthy dishes like this one from China.

INGREDIENTS

8 large open-cap mushrooms
3 scallions, sliced lengthwise
1 garlic clove, crushed
2 tablespoons oyster sauce
10-ounce carton marinated tofu, cut into small dice
7-ounce can corn, drained
2 teaspoon sesame oil
salt and ground black pepper
scallion strips, to garnish

SERVES 4

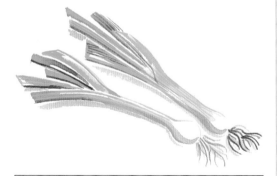

COOK'S TIP
If desired, omit the oyster sauce and use light soy sauce instead.

1 Preheat the oven to 400°F. Set aside the mushroom caps and finely chop the stems. Place the stems in a bowl, add the scallions and garlic and pour in the oyster sauce. Stir to mix.

2 Dry the marinated tofu and add it with the corn to the mushroom mixture, season with salt and pepper, then stir to combine.

3 Place the mushroom caps, open-side up, on a plate or cutting board and divide the stuffing mixture among them.

4 Brush the edges of the mushrooms with the oil. Arrange the mushrooms in a baking dish and bake for 12–15 minutes, until the mushrooms are just tender, then serve garnished with the scallion strips.

MARBLED QUAIL'S EGGS

Hard-boiled quail's eggs reboiled in smoky China tea assume a pretty marbled effect. Dip them into a fragrant spicy salt and pass them with drinks, or serve them as an appetizer. Szechuan peppercorns can be bought at Asian food stores.

INGREDIENTS
12 quail's eggs
2½ cups strong lapsang souchong tea
1 tablespoon dark soy sauce
1 tablespoon dry sherry
2 whole star anise
mixed greens, ground Szechuan peppercorns and sea salt, to serve

SERVES 4–6

1 Place the quail's eggs in a saucepan of cold water and bring to a boil. Time them for 2 minutes from the moment when the water comes to a boil.

2 Transfer the eggs from the pan to a colander and run them under cold water to cool. Tap the shells all over so they are cracked, but do not peel the eggs.

COOK'S TIP
Szechuan peppercorns are dried reddish brown berries from a shrub native to Szechuan. They are not as hot as the true peppercorn, but have a numbing effect and a distinctive aroma. They are roasted, ground, and the husks are discarded before use.

3 In a large saucepan, bring the tea to a boil, then add the soy sauce, sherry and star anise. Add the eggs and boil again for about 15 minutes, partially covered, so the liquid does not boil dry.

4 Remove the eggs from the pan. When they are cool, peel and arrange on a small platter lined with greens.

5 Mix the ground Szechuan peppercorns with an equal amount of salt and place the mixture in a small dish to serve with the eggs.

SHRIMP AND EGG-KNOT SOUP

T here are no set main courses in Japan and all dishes are eaten together. Soup is also eaten for breakfast, when it is typically served with seaweed and a soft-boiled egg.

INGREDIENTS
3¹/₂ cups kombu and bonito stock or instant dashi
1 teaspoon usukuchi *soy sauce*
salt
1 scallion, thinly sliced,
.to garnish

FOR THE SHRIMP SHINJO BALLS
7 ounces raw large shrimp, shelled, thawed if frozen
2¹/₂ ounces cod fillet, skinned
1 teaspoon egg white
1 teaspoon sake or dry white wine, plus an extra dash
4¹/₂ teaspoons cornstarch or potato starch
2–3 drops soy sauce

FOR THE OMELET
1 egg, beaten
dash of mirin
oil, for cooking

SERVES 4

1 Remove the black vein running down the back of the shrimp. Process the shrimp, cod, egg white, the sake or wine, cornstarch or potato starch, soy sauce and a pinch of salt together in a food processor or blender to make a sticky paste. Alternatively, finely chop the shrimp and cod, crush them with the knife's blade and then pound them well in a mortar with a pestle, adding the remaining ingredients.

2 Shape the mixture into four balls and steam for 10 minutes over high heat. Soak the scallion in cold water for 5 minutes, then drain.

3 Mix the egg with a pinch of salt and the mirin. Heat a little oil in a frying pan and pour in the egg, tilting the pan to coat it evenly. When the egg has set, turn the omelet over and cook for 30 seconds. Let cool.

4 Cut the cooked omelet into long strips, each about ³/₄ inch wide. Knot each strip once, place in a strainer and rinse with hot water to remove any excess oil. Bring the stock to a boil and add the *usukuchi* soy sauce, a pinch of salt and a dash of sake or wine.

5 Divide the shrimp balls and the egg knots between four serving bowls. Pour in the soup, sprinkle on the scallions and serve immediately.

SHIITAKE MUSHROOM AND EGG SOUP

O *sumashi* means "clear soup." This Japanese recipe goes particularly well with any sushi, as its delicate flavor complements rather than overpowers the flavor of the fish.

INGREDIENTS
2¹/₂ cups kombu and bonito stock or instant dashi
4 shiitake mushrooms, stems removed, thinly sliced
1 teaspoon salt
2 teaspoons usukuchi soy sauce
1 teaspoon sake or dry white wine
2 eggs
watercress, to garnish

SERVES 4

COOK'S TIP
Shiitake mushrooms can be used to make a delicious stock. Just use the water that you have used to soak them in if they are dried.

1 Bring the stock to a boil, add the shiitake mushrooms and simmer for 1–2 minutes. Do not overcook.

2 Add the salt, *usukuchi* soy sauce and sake or wine. Then break the eggs into a bowl and stir well with chopsticks.

3 Pour the egg into the soup in a thin steady stream, in a circular motion—like you are drawing a spiral shape in the soup. To keep the soup clear, the heat must be high enough to set the egg as soon as it is added.

4 Simmer the soup for a few seconds until the eggs are cooked through. Use a pair of chopsticks to break up the egg in order to divide it equally between four bowls. Remove from heat. Sprinkle on some watercress and serve immediately.

MISO SOUP

This soup is one of the most commonly eaten dishes in Japan, and it is usually served with every meal. Every family has its unique recipe for this soup, with different combinations of ingredients.

INGREDIENTS
5 ounces Japanese silken tofu,
4 x 2 x 1¹/₄ inches
3¹/₂ cups kombu and bonito stock or
instant dashi
¹/₄ ounce dried wakame seaweed
¹/₄ cup white or red miso paste
2 scallions, chopped,
to garnish

SERVES 4

1 Cut the tofu into ½-inch cubes. Bring the stock to a boil and reduce the heat.

2 Add the wakame seaweed and simmer for 1–2 minutes.

3 Pour some soup into a bowl and add the miso paste, stirring until it dissolves, and then pour the mixture back into the pan.

4 Add the tofu and heat through for about 1 minute, then serve immediately, while still very hot. Garnish with the chopped scallions.

COOK'S TIP
Reduce the heat when the stock boils, as it loses flavor if boiled for too long. Similarly, cook the soup long enough to heat the ingredients.

SHRIMP TEMPURA

Tempura is a delicate dish of savory foods in light batter. The secret is to use really cold water and to have the oil at the right temperature.

INGREDIENTS

8 raw jumbo shrimp, heads removed
oil, for deep frying
2¹/₂ ounces daikon, finely grated and drained, and a shiso leaf, to garnish

FOR THE TEMPURA DIP
scant 1 cup water
3 tablespoons mirin
¹/₄ ounce bonito flakes
3 tablespoons soy sauce

FOR THE TEMPURA BATTER
1 egg
6 tablespoons ice water
²/₃ cup all-purpose flour
¹/₂ teaspoon baking powder
2 ice cubes

SERVES 4

COOK'S TIP
Always use Japanese soy sauce in these recipes, as Chinese soy sauce tastes much stronger.

1 Carefully shell the jumbo shrimp, leaving their tails on. Cut one-third of each tail off in a diagonal slit. Press out any excess water with your fingers to prevent it from seeping into the oil and spitting during the cooking process.

2 Make a shallow cut down the back of each shrimp and remove the black intestinal vein.

3 Lay a shrimp on its spine so that it is concave. Using a sharp knife, make three or four diagonal slits into the flesh, about two-thirds of the way in toward the spine, leaving all the pieces attached.

4 Repeat this process with the remaining shrimp. This keeps them straight during cooking. Finally, flatten the shrimp with your fingers.

5 To make the dip, put all the ingredients in a saucepan and bring to a boil. Remove from heat, let cool, and then strain.

6 Slowly heat the oil for deep-frying to 365°F. Start making the batter when the oil is getting warm.

7 Always make the batter just before you use it so that it is still very cold. Stir, but do not beat, the egg in a large bowl and set aside half for another use. Add the ice water, flour and baking powder all at once. Stir only two or three times, ignoring the lumps. Add the ice cubes.

8 Dust the shrimp lightly with flour. Hold one by the tail, quickly coat it with batter and slowly lower it into the oil. Do not drop the shrimp into the oil, as the coating will come off.

9 Repeat with the remaining shrimp, frying them until they rise to the surface of the oil and are crisp. Do not fry until they are golden. Cook a few shrimp at a time and then drain them well. Pour the dip into four small bowls. Place the tempura on a plate, garnish with the daikon and shiso leaf and serve immediately.

SPINACH WITH BONITO FLAKES

T his is a cold side dish of lightly cooked spinach dressed with fine bonito flakes. A similar vegetarian side dish can be prepared by omitting the bonito flakes and marinating the spinach in kombu seaweed dashi and soy sauce.

INGREDIENTS
11 ounces whole spinach, roots trimmed

FOR THE MARINADE
¹/₄ cup kombu and bonito stock or instant dashi
4 teaspoons usukuchi *soy sauce*
4 tablespoons fine bonito flakes
(katsuo bushi)

SERVES 4

1 Wash the spinach thoroughly. Keeping the stems together, hold the leaves of the spinach and lower the stems into boiling water for 10 seconds before lowering the leaves into the water and boiling for 1–2 minutes. Do not overcook.

2 Meanwhile, prepare a large bowl of cold water. Drain the spinach and soak it in the cold water for 1 minute to preserve its color and remove any bitterness.

3 Drain the spinach and squeeze it well, holding the stems upward and squeezing firmly down the length of the spinach leaves.

4 Mix the stock and soy sauce in a dish and marinate the spinach in this mixture for 10–15 minutes, turning it over once.

5 Squeeze the spinach lightly and cut it into 1¼–1½-inch long pieces, reserving the marinade. Divide the spinach among four small bowls, arranging the pieces so that the cut edges face upward. Sprinkle 1 tablespoon bonito flakes and a little of the marinade on each portion, then serve immediately.

DAIKON WITH SESAME MISO SAUCE

This simple vegetable dish makes a good appetizer. The rice is added to keep the daikon white and to remove any bitterness from the vegetables.

INGREDIENTS
1 daikon, about 1³/₄ pounds
1 tablespoon rice, washed
salt, to taste
1 sheet kombu seaweed,
8 x 4 inches
watercress, to garnish

FOR THE SESAME MISO SAUCE
generous ¹/₃ cup each red and white
miso paste
¹/₄ cup mirin
2 tablespoons sugar
4 teaspoons ground white sesame seeds

SERVES 4

1 Slice the daikon into ¾-inch thick slices, then peel off the skin. Wrap the rice in a piece of muslin or cheesecloth and tie with string, allowing room for the rice to expand during cooking. Place the daikon, rice bag and some salt in a pan, fill with water and bring to a boil. Simmer for 15 minutes. Gently drain the daikon and discard the rice.

2 Place the seaweed in a large pan, lay the daikon on top and fill with water. Bring to a boil, then simmer for 20 minutes.

3 Meanwhile, make the sauce. Combine the red and white miso pastes in a saucepan. Add the mirin and sugar, simmer for 5–6 minutes, and make sure that you stir continuously. Remove from heat and add the sesame seeds.

4 Arrange the daikon and seaweed in a large dish with their hot cooking stock. Sprinkle watercress on top. Serve the daikon on small plates with the sesame miso sauce poured on top and garnished with some of the cress. The seaweed is used only to flavor the daikon and is not eaten.

SIMPLE ROLLED SUSHI

To perfect the art of rolling sushi in seaweed, start with this simple form of rolled sushi known as *Hosomaki,* which is usually a slim roll with only one filling. You will need a bamboo mat *(makisu)* for the rolling process.

INGREDIENTS
6 sheets yaki-nori *seaweed*
gari *(ginger pickles), to garnish*
soy sauce, to serve

FOR THE FILLING
7-ounce block tuna for sashimi
7-ounce block salmon for sashimi
2 tablespoons wasabi paste
¹/₂ cucumber, quartered lengthwise and seeds removed

FOR THE RICE
2 cups Japanese rice,
washed and drained for 1 hour
5 teaspoons sake or dry white wine

FOR THE MIXED VINEGAR
10¹/₂ teaspoons rice vinegar
1 tablespoon sugar
²/₃ teaspoon salt

MAKES 12 ROLLS OR 72 SLICES

1 Cook the rice, replacing 5 teaspoons of the measured cooking water with the sake or wine. Heat the ingredients for the vinegar, stir well and cool. Add the rice.

2 Cut the *yaki-nori* in half lengthwise. Cut the fish into four ½-inch square sticks, the length of the long side of the *nori*. Use two sticks per *nori* if necessary.

3 Place a sheet of *nori*, shiny-side facing down, on a bamboo mat on a cutting board.

4 Divide the rice in half in its bowl. Mark each half into six, making 12 portions in all. Spread one portion of the rice onto the *nori* with your fingers, leaving a ½-inch space uncovered at the top and bottom of the *nori*.

5 Spread a little wasabi in a horizontal line along the middle of the rice and lay a stick of tuna on this.

6 Holding the mat and the edge of the *nori* nearest to you, roll up the *nori* and rice into a tube with the tuna in the middle. Use the mat as a guide—do not roll it into the food. Roll the rice tightly so that it sticks together and encloses the filling firmly.

7 Carefully roll the sushi off the mat. Make 11 other rolls in the same way, four for each filling ingredient. Do not use wasabi paste with the cucumber. Use a wet knife to cut each roll into six slices and stand them on a platter. Wipe and re-rinse the knife occasionally between cuts to stop the rice from sticking. Garnish with *gari* and serve soy sauce with the sushi.

YAKITORI CHICKEN

 akitori are Japanese-style chicken kebabs. They are easy to eat and ideal for barbecues or parties.

INGREDIENTS
6 boneless chicken thighs, with skin
bunch of scallions
seven-flavor spice, to serve (optional)

FOR THE YAKITORI SAUCE
$2/3$ cup soy sauce
$1/2$ cup sugar
5 teaspoons sake or dry white wine
1 tablespoon all-purpose flour

SERVES 4

1 To make the sauce, stir the soy sauce, sugar and sake or wine into the flour in a small pan and bring to a boil, stirring. Reduce the heat and simmer for 10 minutes, until the sauce is reduced by one-third. Then set aside.

2 Cut each chicken thigh into six chunks and cut the scallions into 1¼-inch long pieces.

3 Thread the chicken and scallions alternately onto 12 bamboo skewers. Broil under medium heat or cook on the grill, brushing generously several times with the sauce. Broil for 5–10 minutes, until the chicken is cooked but still moist.

4 Serve with a little extra *yakitori* sauce, and sprinkle the kebabs with seven-flavor spice, if desired.

CHICKEN CAKES WITH TERIYAKI SAUCE

hese small chicken cakes, about the size of meatballs, are known in Japanese as *Tsukune*.

INGREDIENTS
14 ounces ground chicken
1 small egg
¹/₄ cup grated onion
1¹/₂ teaspoons sugar
1¹/₂ teaspoons soy sauce
cornstarch, for coating
1 tablespoon oil
*¹/₂ bunch of scallions, finely shredded,
to garnish*

FOR THE TERIYAKI SAUCE
2 tablespoons sake or dry white wine
2 tablespoons sugar
2 tablespoons mirin
2 tablespoons soy sauce

SERVES 4

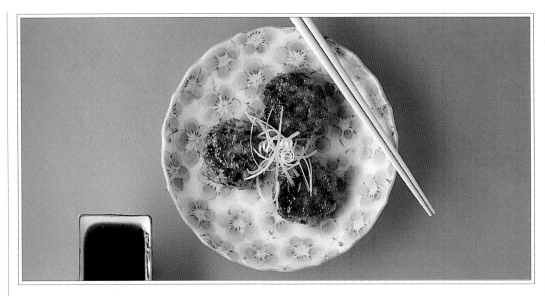

1 Mix the ground chicken with the egg, grated onion, sugar and soy sauce until the ingredients are thoroughly combined and well bound together. This process takes about 3 minutes, until the mixture is quite sticky, which makes for a good texture.

2 Shape the mixture into 12 small, flat round cakes and dust them lightly all over with cornstarch.

3 Soak the scallions in a bowl of cold water for 5 minutes and drain well.

4 Heat the oil in a frying pan. Place the chicken cakes in the pan in a single layer, and cook them over medium heat for 3 minutes. Turn the cakes over and cook for 3 minutes on the second side.

5 Mix the ingredients for the sauce and pour into the frying pan. Turn the chicken cakes occasionally until they are evenly glazed with the sauce. Move or gently shake the pan constantly to prevent the sauce from burning.

6 Arrange the chicken cakes on a serving plate and top them with the shredded scallions. Serve immediately.

SEAFOOD DISHES

Fish and seafood are vital parts of Asian cooking, since many of these countries have extensive coastlines. The freshest seafood is combined with the freshest spices and vegetables, and cooked in the minimum time to preserve the most flavor. Fish and coconut are a favorite combination in Asian cooking, used in curries such as Kashmir Coconut Fish and in peanut sauce for Sate Shrimp.

In Chinese dishes the fish is quickly stir-fried with ginger and scallions, soy sauce and rice wine. Japanese cooking relies on the freshest fish of all, often using raw or lightly marinated tuna, salmon and seafood to make the classic dishes sushi and sashimi.

GRILLED FISH MASALA

These tasty fish fillets with their spicy coating are very simple to prepare. They are cooked using a minimum of oil, so are a healthy option.

INGREDIENTS
4 flat fish fillets, such as sole or flounder, about 4 ounces each

FOR THE SPICE MIXTURE
1 garlic clove, crushed
1 teaspoon garam masala
1 teaspoon chili powder
¼ teaspoon ground turmeric
½ teaspoon salt
1 tablespoon finely chopped cilantro
1 tablespoon vegetable oil
2 tablespoons lemon juice
grated carrot, tomato quarters and lime slices, to garnish

SERVES 4

1 Line a flameproof dish or broiler pan with aluminum foil. Rinse the fish fillets under cold running water, pat dry with paper towels and put them into the dish or pan.

2 To make the spice mixture, put the crushed garlic clove and garam masala into a small bowl. Stir in the chili powder, ground turmeric, the salt and the finely chopped cilantro. Gradually add the vegetable oil, stirring constantly. Add the lemon juice and stir thoroughly to mix, then set the spice mixture aside. Preheat the broiler to very hot.

3 Lower the temperature of the broiler to medium. Using a pastry brush, baste the fish fillets evenly all over with the spice mixture. Broil the fish fillets on each side for about 5 minutes, basting occasionally with the juices that form in the pan, until they are cooked through.

4 To serve, transfer the fish fillets to a warmed serving platter and make a decorative garnish with the grated carrot, tomato quarters and lime slices. Serve immediately, with naan, if desired.

COOK'S TIP
For a stronger flavor, brush the fish fillets with the spice mixture an hour or so before you broil them to let the spices permeate the flesh.

FISH IN COCONUT SAUCE

U se fresh fish fillets to make this dish if you can, as they have much more flavor than frozen ones. If you are using frozen fillets, ensure that they are completely thawed before cooking.

INGREDIENTS
2 tablespoons corn oil
1 teaspoon onion seeds
4 dried red chiles, crumbled
3 garlic cloves, sliced
1 onion, sliced
2 tomatoes
2 tablespoons dry, shredded coconut
1 teaspoon salt
1 teaspoon ground cilantro
4 flat fish fillets, such as sole or flounder,
about 3 ounces each
⅔ cup water
1 tablespoon lime juice
1 tablespoon chopped cilantro
rice or parathas, to serve

SERVES 4

1 Heat the oil in a deep, round frying pan or a karahi. Lower the heat slightly and add the onion seeds, dried red chiles, garlic and onion. Cook the mixture for 3–4 minutes, stirring once or twice.

2 Cut a cross on the base of each tomato. Plunge the tomatoes into a bowl of boiling water for 20–30 seconds, then into a bowl of cold water. Peel off the skins, then slice thinly. Add the tomatoes, coconut, salt and ground cilantro to the pan and stir to mix thoroughly.

3 Cut each fish fillet into three pieces. Drop the fish pieces into the onion and tomato mixture and turn them gently until they are well coated.

4 Cook for 5–7 minutes, lowering the heat if necessary. Add the measured water, lime juice and chopped cilantro and cook for another 3–5 minutes, until the water has almost all evaporated. Serve the fish with rice or parathas.

COOK'S TIP
Balti is the name of both a deep, round frying pan with two ring handles, and the dish cooked in it. Also known as a karahi, the Balti pan is very similar to a wok, which makes an excellent substitute.

KASHMIR COCONUT FISH

Fish and coconut are a popular combination in Asian cooking. This deliciously sweet curry can be served with rice or naan.

INGREDIENTS
2 tablespoons vegetable oil
2 onions, sliced
1 green bell pepper, seeded and sliced
1 garlic clove, crushed
1 dried chile, seeded and chopped
1 teaspoon ground cilantro
1 teaspoon ground cumin
½ teaspoon ground turmeric
½ teaspoon hot chili powder
½ teaspoon garam masala
1 tablespoon all-purpose flour
1⅓ cups coconut milk
1½ pounds haddock fillet,
skinned and chopped
4 tomatoes, skinned, seeded and chopped
1 tablespoon lemon juice
2 tablespoons ground almonds
2 tablespoons heavy cream
salt and freshly ground black pepper
cilantro sprigs, to garnish
naan and rice, to serve

SERVES 4

1 Heat the oil in a large saucepan and add the onions, pepper and garlic. Cook for 6–7 minutes, until the onions and peppers have softened. Stir in the chopped dried chile, all the ground spices, the chili powder, garam masala and flour, and cook for 1 minute.

2 Add the coconut milk to 2½ cups boiling water and stir into the spicy vegetable mixture. Bring to a boil, cover and then simmer gently for 6 minutes.

3 Add the fish and tomatoes and cook for 5–6 minutes or until the fish has turned opaque. Uncover and gently stir in the lemon juice, ground almonds and cream. Season well and garnish with cilantro.

COOK'S TIP
You can replace the haddock with other firm-fleshed white fish, such as cod or whiting, or even stir in a few cooked peeled shrimp, if desired.

FISH IN BANANA LEAVES

Fish that is prepared in this way is particularly succulent and flavorful. Fillets are used here rather than whole fish—easier for those who don't like to mess about with bones. It is a great dish for barbecues and grills.

INGREDIENTS

1 cup coconut milk
2 tablespoons red curry paste
3 tablespoons fish sauce
2 tablespoons sugar
5 kaffir lime leaves, torn
6 ounces fish fillets, such
as snapper
6 ounces mixed vegetables, such as
carrots or leeks, finely shredded
4 banana leaves
2 tablespoons shredded scallions,
and 2 red chiles, finely sliced,
to garnish

SERVES 4

1 Combine the coconut milk, curry paste, fish sauce, sugar and kaffir lime leaves in a shallow dish.

2 Marinate the fish in this mixture for 15–30 minutes. Preheat the oven to 400°F.

3 Combine the vegetables and lay a portion on top of a banana leaf. Place a piece of fish on top, together with a little of its marinade.

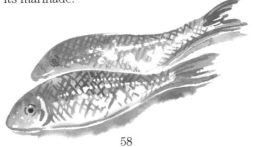

4 Wrap the fish up by turning in the sides and ends of the leaf and secure with toothpicks. Repeat with the rest of the leaves and fish.

5 Bake for 20–25 minutes or until the fish is cooked. Alternatively, cook under the broiler or on a grill. Just before serving, garnish with a sprinkling of scallions and sliced red chiles.

CURRIED SHRIMP IN COCONUT MILK

 curry-like dish from Thailand where the shrimp are cooked in a wonderful spicy coconut sauce.

INGREDIENTS

2½ cups coconut milk
2 tablespoons yellow curry paste
(see Cook's Tip)
1 tablespoon fish sauce
½ teaspoon salt
1 teaspoon granulated sugar
1 pound jumbo shrimp, shelled, tails left intact and deveined
8 ounces cherry tomatoes
juice of ½ lime, to serve
2 red chiles, cut into strips, and cilantro leaves, to garnish

SERVES 4–6

1 Put half the coconut milk into a pan or wok and bring to a boil.

2 Add the yellow curry paste to the coconut milk, stir until it disperses, then simmer for about 10 minutes.

3 Add the fish sauce, salt, sugar and remaining coconut milk. Simmer for another 5 minutes.

4 Add the shrimp and cherry tomatoes. Simmer gently for about 5 minutes until the shrimp are pink and tender.

5 Serve sprinkled with lime juice and garnished with chiles and cilantro.

COOK'S TIP
To make yellow curry paste, process together 6–8 yellow chiles, 1 chopped lemongrass stalk, 4 peeled shallots, 4 garlic cloves, 1 tablespoon peeled chopped ginger root, 1 teaspoon cilantro seeds, 1 teaspoon mustard powder, 1 teaspoon salt, ½ teaspoon ground cinnamon, 1 tablespoon light brown sugar and 2 tablespoons oil in a food processor. When a paste has formed, transfer to a glass jar and chill.

SATE SHRIMP

n enticing and tasty dish. Lightly cooked greens and jasmine rice make good accompaniments.

INGREDIENTS
*1 pound jumbo shrimp, shelled, tail ends
left intact and deveined
½ bunch cilantro leaves, 4 red chiles,
finely sliced, and scallions, cut
diagonally, to garnish*

FOR THE PEANUT SAUCE
*3 tablespoons vegetable oil
1 tablespoon chopped garlic
1 small onion, chopped
3–4 red chiles, crushed and chopped
3 kaffir lime leaves, torn
1 lemongrass stalk, bruised
and chopped
1 teaspoon medium curry paste
1 cup coconut milk
½-inch piece cinnamon stick
3 ounces crunchy peanut butter
3 tablespoons tamarind juice
2 tablespoons fish sauce
2 tablespoons sugar
juice of ½ lemon*

SERVES 4–6

1 To make the sauce, heat half the oil in a wok or large frying pan and add the garlic and onion. Cook until it softens, 3–4 minutes.

2 Add the chiles, kaffir lime leaves, lemongrass and curry paste. Cook for another 2–3 minutes.

3 Stir in the coconut milk, cinnamon stick, peanut butter, tamarind juice, fish sauce, sugar and lemon juice.

4 Reduce the heat and simmer gently for 15–20 minutes, until the sauce thickens, stirring occasionally to ensure that the sauce doesn't stick to the bottom of the wok or frying pan.

5 Heat the rest of the oil in a wok or large frying pan. Add the shrimp and stir-fry for 3–4 minutes or until the shrimp turn pink and are slightly firm to the touch.

6 Mix the shrimp with the sauce. Serve garnished with cilantro leaves, red chiles and scallions.

THAI SHRIMP SALAD

his salad has the distinctive flavor of lemongrass, an ingredient used widely in Southeast Asian cooking.

INGREDIENTS

*9 ounces cooked, peeled
extra large jumbo shrimp
1 tablespoon fish sauce
2 tablespoons lime juice
½ teaspoon light brown sugar
1 small fresh red chile, finely chopped
1 scallion, finely chopped
1 small garlic clove, crushed
1-inch piece fresh lemongrass,
finely chopped
2 tablespoons chopped cilantro
3 tablespoons dry white wine
8–12 lettuce leaves, to serve
cilantro sprigs, to garnish*

SERVES 4

1 Place the shrimp in a bowl and add the fish sauce, lime juice, sugar, chile, scallion, garlic and lemongrass. Stir together, and then add the cilantro and wine. Stir well, cover and let marinate in the refrigerator for 2–3 hours until the flavors have permeated the shrimp. Mix and turn the shrimp occasionally, so that they are evenly coated.

2 Arrange two or three of the lettuce leaves on four serving plates.

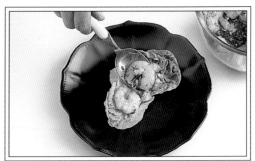

3 Spoon the shrimp salad into the lettuce leaves. Garnish with cilantro and serve immediately.

STIR-FRIED SCALLOPS WITH ASPARAGUS

A sparagus is extremely popular in China and Thailand. The combination of garlic and black pepper gives this dish its spiciness. You can replace the scallops with shrimp or some other firm variety of seafood.

INGREDIENTS
4 tablespoons vegetable oil
1 bunch asparagus, cut into
2-inch lengths
4 garlic cloves, finely chopped
2 shallots, finely chopped
1 pound scallops, cleaned
2 tablespoons fish sauce
½ teaspoon coarsely ground
black pepper
½ cup coconut milk
cilantro leaves, to garnish

SERVES 4–6

1 Heat half the oil in a wok or large frying pan. Add the asparagus and stir-fry for about 2 minutes. Transfer the asparagus to a plate and set aside.

2 Add the rest of the oil, garlic and shallots to the same wok and stir-fry until fragrant. Add the scallops, stir and cook for another 1–2 minutes.

3 Return the asparagus to the wok. Add the fish sauce, ground black pepper and coconut milk.

4 Stir and cook for another 3–4 minutes or until the scallops and asparagus are cooked. Garnish with the cilantro leaves.

MALAYSIAN FISH CURRY

T his potent curry, known as *Ikan Moolee,* is often served with Hot Tomato Sambal and plain rice.

INGREDIENTS

1¹/₂ pounds monkfish, or
red snapper fillet
3 tablespoons freshly grated
or dry shredded coconut
2 tablespoons vegetable oil
1 piece galangal *or fresh ginger root,*
1 inch long, peeled and thinly sliced
2 small red chiles, seeded
and finely chopped
2 cloves garlic, crushed
1 piece lemongrass,
2 inches long, shredded
1 piece shrimp paste, ¹/₂-inch square,
or 1 tablespoon fish sauce
1²/₃ cups canned coconut milk
2¹/₂ cups chicken stock
¹/₂ teaspoon turmeric
1 tablespoon sugar
juice of 1 lime or ¹/₂ lemon
salt
chunks of lime, freshly chopped cilantro
Hot Tomato Sambal, to serve

SERVES 4–6

1 Cut the fish into large chunks, season with salt and set aside.

2 Dry-fry the coconut in a wok until evenly brown. Add the oil, *galangal* or ginger, chiles, garlic and lemongrass and fry briefly. Stir in the shrimp paste or fish sauce. Strain the coconut milk through a sieve, and add the thin coconut liquid.

3 Add the chicken stock, turmeric, sugar, a little salt and the lime or lemon juice. Simmer for 10 minutes. Add the fish and simmer for another 6–8 minutes. Stir in the solid from the coconut milk, and simmer gently to thicken. Transfer to a large bowl. Decorate with lime and cilantro to serve.

CHILI CRABS

It is possible to find variations on *Kepitang Pedas*, as it's called in Indonesia, all over Asia.

INGREDIENTS
2 cooked crabs, about 1½ pounds
½-inch cube terasi
2 garlic cloves
2 fresh red chiles, seeded, or 1 teaspoon chopped chile from a jar
1-inch piece fresh ginger root, peeled and sliced
¼ cup sunflower oil
1¼ cups ketchup
1 tablespoon dark brown sugar
⅔ cup warm water
4 scallions, chopped, to garnish
cucumber chunks and hot toast, to serve (optional)

SERVES 4

1 Remove the large claws of one crab and turn it onto its back, with the head facing away from you. Push the body up from the main shell. Discard the stomach sac, lungs and any green matter. Leave the brown meat in the shell and cut in half with a cleaver. Cut the body section in half and crack the claws with a sharp blow from a hammer or cleaver. Avoid splintering the claws. Repeat with the other crab.

2 Grind the *terasi,* garlic, chiles and ginger into a paste in a food processor or with a pestle and mortar.

3 Heat a wok or heavy pan and add the oil. Fry the spice paste, stirring constantly, without browning.

4 Stir in the ketchup, sugar and water and mix well. When just boiling, add the crab pieces and toss in the sauce until well coated and hot. Serve in a large bowl, sprinkled with the chopped scallions. Place in the center of the table for everyone to help themselves. Accompany with cucumber chunks and hot toast, if using, for mopping up the sauce.

STIR-FRIED SEAFOOD

A colorful and delicious dish from Southeast China, combining shrimp, squid, and scallops. The squid may be replaced by another fish, or omitted altogether.

INGREDIENTS
4 ounces squid, cleaned
4–6 fresh scallops
4 ounces uncooked shrimp
½ egg white
1 tablespoon cornstarch, mixed with a little water
2–3 celery stalks
1 small red bell pepper, cored and seeded
2 small carrots
1¼ cups oil
½ teaspoon finely chopped fresh ginger root
1 scallion, cut into short sections
1 teaspoon salt
½ teaspoon light brown sugar
1 tablespoon Chinese rice wine or dry sherry
1 tablespoon light soy sauce
1 teaspoon hot bean sauce
2 tablespoons chicken stock
few drops of sesame oil, to serve

SERVES 4

1 Open up the squid and, using a sharp knife, score the inside in a criss-cross pattern. Cut the squid into ½-inch pieces. Soak the squid in a bowl of boiling water until all the pieces curl up; rinse in cold water and drain.

2 Cut each scallop into 3–4 slices. Peel the shrimp and cut each one in half lengthwise. In a bowl, mix the scallops and shrimp with the egg white and cornstarch paste until well blended.

3 Cut the celery, red pepper and carrots into ½–1-inch slices.

4 Heat a wok, then add the oil. When it is medium-hot, add the seafood and stir-fry for 30–40 seconds. Remove with a large slotted spoon and drain.

5 Pour off the excess oil, leaving about 2 tablespoons in the wok, and add the vegetables with the ginger and scallion. Stir-fry for about 1 minute.

6 Return the seafood to the wok, stir for another 30–40 seconds, then stir in the salt, sugar, wine or sherry, soy sauce and hot bean sauce. Add the stock and stir for about 1 minute. Serve sprinkled with sesame oil.

SHRIMP FU-YUNG

This is a very colorful dish that is simple to make. Most of the preparation can be done well in advance. It comes from the south of China.

INGREDIENTS
3 eggs, beaten, reserving 1 teaspoon of egg white
1 teaspoon salt
1 tablespoon finely chopped scallions
3–4 tablespoons vegetable oil
8 ounces uncooked shrimp, peeled
2 teaspoons cornstarch, mixed with a little water
6 ounces peas
1 tablespoon Chinese rice wine or dry sherry

SERVES 4

1 Beat the eggs with a pinch of the salt, and a little of the scallion. In a wok, scramble the eggs in a little oil over medium heat. Remove and reserve.

2 Mix the shrimp with a little of the salt, the egg white, and the cornstarch paste. Heat the oil in a wok. When it is hot, add the peas and stir-fry for 30 seconds. Add the shrimp.

3 Add the scallions, and stir-fry for another minute, then stir the mixture into the scrambled eggs with the last of the salt and the wine or sherry. Blend well and serve immediately.

BRAISED FISH WITH MUSHROOMS

This is a Chinese version of the French *filets de sole bonne femme* (sole with mushrooms and wine sauce), with Asian flavors.

INGREDIENTS

1 pound fillets of lemon sole or flounder
½ egg white
2 tablespoons cornstarch, mixed with a little water
2½ cups vegetable oil
1 tablespoon finely chopped scallions
½ teaspoon finely chopped fresh ginger root
4 ounces white mushrooms, thinly sliced
1 teaspoon light brown sugar
1 tablespoon light soy sauce
2 tablespoons Chinese rice wine or dry sherry
1 tablespoon brandy
½ cup chicken stock
salt
few drops of sesame oil, to serve

SERVES 4

1 Trim off the soft bones along the edge of the fish, but leave the skin on. Cut each fillet into bite-size pieces. Put a little salt, the egg white and about half of the cornstarch paste into a small bowl and combine. Coat the fish pieces in the mixture.

2 Heat the oil in a wok until medium-hot, add the fish pieces one at a time and stir gently so they do not stick. Remove after about 1 minute and drain. Pour off all but 2 tablespoons of oil. Stir-fry the scallions, ginger and mushrooms for 1 minute.

3 Add the sugar, light soy sauce, rice wine or sherry, the brandy and stock and bring to a boil. Add the fish pieces and braise for 1 minute. Thicken with the remaining cornstarch paste and sprinkle with sesame oil. Serve immediately.

FIVE-SPICE FISH

C hinese mixtures of spicy, sweet and sour flavors are particularly successful with fish, and dinner will be ready in minutes.

INGREDIENTS
4 white fish fillets, such as cod, haddock or flounder, about 6 ounces each
1 teaspoon five-spice powder
4 teaspoons cornstarch
1 tablespoon sesame or sunflower oil
3 scallions, finely sliced
1 teaspoon finely chopped fresh ginger root
5 ounces button mushrooms, sliced
4 ounces baby corn, sliced
2 tablespoons soy sauce
3 tablespoons dry sherry or apple juice
1 teaspoon sugar
salt and ground black pepper
stir-fried vegetables, to serve

SERVES 4

1 Toss the fish fillets in the five-spice powder and cornstarch to coat.

2 Heat the oil in a wok or frying pan and stir-fry the scallions, ginger, mushrooms and corn for about 1 minute. Add the fish fillets and cook for 2–3 minutes, turning once.

3 In a small bowl, combine the soy sauce, sherry or juice and sugar, then pour onto the fish. Simmer for 2 minutes, season, then serve immediately with stir-fried vegetables.

STEAMED FISH WITH GINGER

A ny firm-fleshed fish with a delicate taste, such as salmon or turbot, can be cooked by this method. The sweet taste of ginger root combined with scallions makes this dish a favorite on mainland China.

INGREDIENTS
1 sea bass, trout or snapper, weighing
about 1½ pounds, cleaned
½ teaspoon salt
1 tablespoon sesame oil
2–3 scallions, cut in half lengthwise
2 tablespoons light soy sauce
2 tablespoons Chinese rice wine or
dry sherry
1 tablespoon finely grated
ginger root
2 tablespoons vegetable oil
finely shredded scallions, to garnish

SERVES 4–6

1 Using a sharp knife, score both sides of the fish as far down as the bone, making several diagonal cuts about 1 inch apart. Rub the fish all over, inside and out, with salt and sesame oil.

2 Sprinkle the scallions evenly on a heatproof platter and place the fish on top. Blend the soy sauce and wine or sherry with the ginger and pour onto the fish.

3 Place the platter in a steamer over boiling water (or inside a wok on a rack), and steam vigorously, covered, for 12–15 minutes, until the fish is cooked *(left)*.

4 Heat the oil in a small saucepan; remove the platter from the steamer, place the shredded scallions on top of the fish, then pour the hot oil along the whole length of the fish. Serve immediately.

RED AND WHITE SHRIMP

T he Chinese name for this dish is Yuan Yang Shrimp. Pairs of Mandarin ducks are also known as *Yuan Yang,* or love birds, because they are always seen together. They symbolize affection and happiness.

INGREDIENTS
1 pound uncooked shrimp
pinch of salt
½ egg white
1 tablespoon cornstarch, mixed with a little water
6 ounces snowpeas
2½ cups vegetable oil
½ teaspoon salt
1 teaspoon light brown sugar
1 tablespoon finely chopped scallions
1 teaspoon finely chopped fresh ginger root
1 tablespoon light soy sauce
1 tablespoon Chinese rice wine or dry sherry
1 teaspoon hot bean sauce
1 tablespoon tomato paste

SERVES 4–6

1 Peel and devein the shrimp, and mix with the salt, egg white and cornstarch paste. Trim the snowpeas.

2 Heat a wok, then add 2–3 tablespoons of the oil. When it is hot, add the snowpeas and stir-fry for about 1 minute, then add the salt and sugar and continue stirring for another minute. Remove the snowpeas with a slotted spoon and place in the center of a warmed serving platter.

3 Heat the remaining oil, partially cook the shrimp for 1 minute, remove, and drain on paper towels.

4 Pour off the excess oil, leaving about 1 tablespoon in the wok, and add the scallions, ginger and shrimp. Stir-fry for 1 minute, then add the soy sauce and wine or sherry. Blend well and place half of the shrimp at one end of the platter.

5 Add the hot bean sauce and tomato paste to the remaining shrimp. Blend well and place the "red" shrimp at the other end of the platter. Serve immediately.

TUNA RICE BOWL

One of the most popular dishes in Japan, *Tekka-don* consists of rice with fresh tuna laid on top.

INGREDIENTS
2¹/₄ cups Japanese rice, washed and drained for 1 hour
2 tablespoons sake or dry white wine
11-ounce block tuna for sashimi
1 sheet yaki-nori seaweed
4 teaspoons wasabi paste,
to garnish
soy sauce, to serve

SERVES 4

1 Cook the rice, replacing 2 tablespoons of the measured cooking water with the sake or wine.

2 Cut thin slices of tuna, tilting the block to the side. Cut toward you from the far side.

3 Using scissors, cut the *yaki-nori* seaweed very carefully into 2-inch size pieces.

4 The rice must be at room temperature, so as not to cook the tuna. Divide it between four bowls.

5 Arrange the tuna on top of the rice and sprinkle the seaweed gently on top. Garnish with lettuce and 1 teaspoon of the wasabi paste for each plate, and serve immediately with soy sauce.

SLICED RAW SALMON

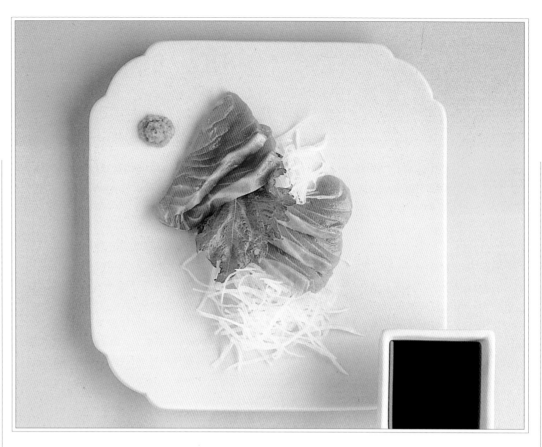

Sliced fresh fish is known as sashimi in Japan. This recipe introduces the cutting technique known as *hira zukuri*. Salmon is a good choice for those who have not tried sashimi before because most people are familiar with smoked salmon, which is also uncooked.

INGREDIENTS
2 fresh salmon fillets, skinned and any bones removed, about 14 ounces total weight
soy sauce, to serve

FOR THE GARNISH
¼ cup daikon
4 teaspoons wasabi paste
shiso leaf

SERVES 4

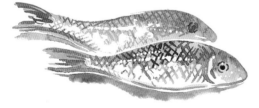

1 Put the salmon fillets in a freezer for about 10 minutes to make them easier to cut, then lay them skinned-side up with the thick end to your right and away from you. Tilt the fish to the left.

2 Carefully, slice the fish toward you, starting the cut from the point of the knife, then slide the slice away from the fillet, to the right. Always slice from the far side toward you.

3 Using a sharp knife, finely shred the daikon. Place it in a large bowl of cold water and let it sit for about 5 minutes, then drain it well.

4 Place three slices of prepared salmon on a serving plate, then overlap another two slices on them diagonally. You can arrange fewer or more slices per portion, but an odd number looks better.

5 Garnish each plate of salmon with the finely shredded daikon, wasabi paste and a shiso leaf, then serve the dish immediately with a small bowl of soy sauce for dipping.

SHAPED SUSHI

his exciting and fresh sushi dish includes some sashimi, which are slices of raw fish.

INGREDIENTS
2¹/₄ cups Japanese rice, washed and drained for 1 hour
2 tablespoons sake or dry white wine
1 rolled omelet
1 teaspoon wasabi paste
soy sauce, gari and lettuce, to serve

FOR THE SUSHI VINEGAR
¹/₄ cup rice vinegar
1 tablespoon sugar
1 teaspoon salt

FOR THE SEAFOOD GARNISH
1 squid body sack, skinned, about 7 ounces total weight
1 leg boiled octopus
7-ounce block tuna for sashimi
7-ounce block salmon for sashimi
4 raw shrimp with shells, heads removed

FOR THE MARINADE
1 tablespoon rice vinegar
1 teaspoon sugar
pinch of salt

SERVES 4

1 Cook the rice, replacing 2 tablespoons of the measured cooking water with the sake or wine.

2 Meanwhile, heat the ingredients for the sushi vinegar, stir well and cool. Add this to the hot cooked rice, stir well with a spatula, at the same time fanning the rice constantly—this gives the rice an attractive glaze. Cover with a damp dish cloth and let cool. Do not put in the refrigerator, as this will make the rice hard.

3 Cut the squid into strips measuring ³/₄–1¹/₄ inches wide and 2 inches long. Carefully, slice the octopus leg into strips of the same size. Cut the blocks of tuna and salmon into ¹/₈-inch thick pieces.

4 Thread the shrimp on bamboo skewers from tail to head to make sure they lie flat when cooked. Boil for 1 minute, then remove the skewers and shells, leaving the tails intact. Slit each shrimp along the belly, taking care not to cut through, and remove the dark vein. Open each one up like a book.

5 Mix the marinade ingredients in a dish, add the shrimp and set aside for about 10 minutes.

6 Slice the rolled omelet into ¹/₄-inch thick pieces.

7 Wet your hands with some cold water, and then carefully shape ¹/₂–³/₄ ounces rice into a rectangle measuring ¹/₂ inches high, ³/₄ inches wide and 2 inches long. Repeat this process with the remaining rice.

8 Use your finger to spread a little wasabi paste onto the middle of each rice rectangle, and divide the seafood among the rectangles, laying them on top. Do not add wasabi paste for egg sushi.

9 Serve the sushi immediately, with soy sauce, *gari* and lettuce. The *gari* may be eaten to cleanse the palate after each mouthful, if desired.

SALMON SEALED WITH EGG

Tamago-toji, meaning egg cover, is the Japanese title for this type of dish which can be made from various ingredients. Canned pink salmon is used here for a very delicate flavor. Fried tofu can be used instead of salmon.

INGREDIENTS
*14-ounce can pink salmon, drained,
bones and skin removed
10 snowpeas, trimmed
2 large mild onions, sliced
8 teaspoons sugar
2 tablespoons soy sauce
4 small eggs, beaten*

SERVES 4

1 Flake the canned salmon. Boil the trimmed snowpeas for 2–3 minutes, drain and slice finely.

2 Put the sliced onions in a frying pan, add scant 1 cup water and bring to a boil. Cook for 5 minutes over medium heat, then add the sugar and soy sauce. Cook for another 5 minutes.

3 Add the flaked salmon and cook for 2–3 minutes or until the soup has virtually evaporated. Pour on the egg to cover the surface. Sprinkle in the snowpeas and cover the pan. Cook for 1 minute over medium heat, until just set. Do not overcook, or the eggs will curdle and separate. Spoon onto a plate from the pan and serve immediately.

FRIED SWORDFISH

T his is a light and tasty cold dish that is suitable for serving on a hot summer's day. Dashi is a stock that provides the underlying flavor for most Japanese dishes.

INGREDIENTS
4 swordfish steaks, boned, skin left on,
about 1 pound 5 ounces total weight
1 tablespoon soy sauce
1½ teaspoons rice vinegar
bunch of scallions
4 asparagus spears, trimmed
2 tablespoons oil

FOR THE MARINADE
3 tablespoons soy sauce
3 tablespoons rice vinegar
2 tablespoons sake or dry white wine
1 tablespoon sugar
1 tablespoon instant dashi or water
1½ teaspoons sesame oil

SERVES 4

1 Cut the swordfish steaks into 1½-inch chunks and place in a dish. Pour the 1 tablespoon soy sauce and 1½ teaspoons rice vinegar onto the fish, then set aside for about 5 minutes. Meanwhile, cut the scallions into 1¼-inch lengths and the asparagus spears into 1½-inch lengths.

2 Mix the ingredients for the marinade in a dish. Heat three-quarters of the oil in a frying pan. Wipe the swordfish with paper towels and fry over medium heat for 1–2 minutes on each side or until cooked. Remove the fish from the frying pan and place it in the marinade.

3 Clean the frying pan and heat the remaining oil in it. Fry the scallions over medium heat, until browned, then add them to the fish. Cook the asparagus in the oil remaining in the pan over low heat for 3–4 minutes, then add to the fish.

4 Let the fish and vegetables marinate for 10–20 minutes, turning the pieces occasionally. Serve the cold fish with the marinade on a large, deep plate.

POACHED MACKEREL WITH MISO

This dish, *Mackerel Miso-ni*, is typical of Japanese-style home cooking. There are many types of Japanese miso bean paste, including white miso, which is sweet in flavor and dark miso, which tastes salty. Darker miso is preferred for this recipe, but you can use any type.

INGREDIENTS
1 mackerel, gutted, 1¹/₂–1³/₄ pounds
1¹/₄ cups instant dashi
2 tablespoons sugar
¹/₄ cup sake or dry white wine
¹/₄ ounce fresh ginger root, peeled and finely sliced
¹/₂ cup miso
¹/₄ ounce fresh ginger root, peeled and finely shredded, to garnish

SERVES 4

COOK'S TIP
When boiling fish, gently lower it into boiling water. Do not add it to cold water, as the fish will smell unpleasant and the cooking liquid or soup will taste bitter.

1 Chop the head off the mackerel and cut the fish into ¾-inch thick steaks. Soak the shredded ginger for the garnish in cold water for 5 minutes, then drain well.

2 Fold a sheet of aluminum foil just smaller than the diameter of a large shallow pan. Pour the dashi, sugar and sake or wine into the pan. Bring to a boil, then arrange the mackerel in the pan in a single layer and add the sliced ginger. Spoon the soup onto the mackerel, then place the foil over it. Simmer the mackerel for 5–6 minutes.

3 Dissolve the miso in a small mixing bowl in a little of the soup liquid from the saucepan. Carefully pour it back into the saucepan and simmer for 12 more minutes, spooning the soup onto the mackerel occasionally as it cooks.

4 Use a slotted spoon to remove the mackerel carefully from the saucepan and place it on a serving plate. Spoon the remaining soup on top and garnish the dish with the finely shredded ginger. Serve the mackerel hot.

TERIYAKI TROUT

Teriyaki sauce is very useful, not only for fish but also for meat. It is a delicious sweet soy-based sauce that creates a lovely shiny gloss that is very attractive.

INGREDIENTS
4 trout fillets

FOR THE TERIYAKI MARINADE
5 tablespoons soy sauce
5 tablespoons sake or dry white wine
5 tablespoons mirin

SERVES 4

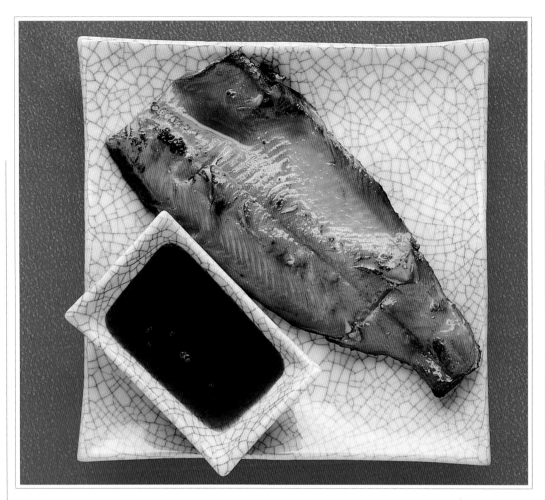

1 Lay the fillets in a shallow dish in a single layer. Mix the marinade ingredients and pour onto the fish. Cover and marinate in the refrigerator for 5–6 hours. Turn occasionally.

2 Thread two trout fillets neatly together on two metal skewers. Repeat with the remaining two fillets. You can cut the fillets in half if they are too big.

3 Cook the trout fillets on a grill over high heat. Be sure to keep the fish about 4 inches away from the flames and brush it with the marinade several times during cooking. Grill each side of the fish until shiny and the trout is cooked through. Alternatively, cook the trout under the broiler.

4 Slide the trout off the metal skewers while it is still hot. Serve the fillets either hot or cold with any remaining marinade poured on top.

POULTRY DISHES

Chicken lends itself perfectly to stir-frying, one of the most popular forms of Asian cooking. The Chinese use a wok to stir-fry their dishes, cutting both meat and vegetables into small pieces and cooking them at high temperatures to retain their flavor and vitamins.

Balti cooking uses a karahi, an Indian version of the wok, to make delicious combinations of poultry, vegetables and spices. Try Poussins in Tamarind Sauce for an unusual combination of sweet, sour and spicy flavors. Chicken salad may not sound like an Asian dish but this section includes three delicious varieties. Tangy Chicken Salad, Chiang Mai Salad and Hot-and-Sour Chicken Salad, all three from Vietnam and Thailand, elevate this humble dish to something very special.

KHARA MASALA CHICKEN

W hole spices (*khara*) are used in this recipe, giving it a wonderfully rich flavor. This is a dry dish, so it is best served with raita and parathas.

INGREDIENTS

¼ teaspoon mustard seeds
¼ teaspoon each fennel and onion seeds
2 curry leaves
½ teaspoon crushed dried red chiles
½ teaspoon white cumin seeds
¼ teaspoon fenugreek seeds
½ teaspoon crushed pomegranate seeds
1 teaspoon salt
1 teaspoon sliced fresh ginger root
3 garlic cloves, sliced
¼ cup corn oil
4 large fresh green chiles, slit
1 large onion, sliced
1 tomato, sliced
1½ pounds chicken, skinned, boned and cubed
chopped cilantro, to garnish

SERVES 4

1 Combine the mustard, fennel and onion seeds, curry leaves, crushed red chiles, cumin seeds, fenugreek seeds, crushed pomegranate seeds and salt in a large bowl, then add the ginger and garlic.

2 Heat the oil in a medium karahi or deep round frying pan and stir in the spice mixture and green chiles. Add the onion and cook over medium heat, stirring occasionally for 5–7 minutes, until the onion is soft and translucent.

3 Add the tomato and chicken pieces to the karahi and cook over medium heat for about 7 minutes or until the chicken is cooked through and the sauce has thickened and reduced.

4 Stir the tomato and chicken mixture together thoroughly and continue cooking over low heat for another 3–5 minutes, until most of the sauce has reduced. Garnish the chicken with chopped cilantro and serve immediately.

CHILI CHICKEN

Hot and spicy is the best way of describing this dish. The aroma of the fresh chiles cooking is truly mouthwatering!

INGREDIENTS

5 tablespoons corn oil
8 large fresh green chiles, slit
½ teaspoon mixed onion and
cumin seeds
4 curry leaves
1 teaspoon sliced fresh ginger root
1 teaspoon chili powder
1 teaspoon ground cilantro
1 garlic clove, crushed
1 teaspoon salt
2 onions, chopped
1½ pounds chicken, skinned, boned
and cubed
1 tablespoon lemon juice
1 tablespoon roughly chopped fresh mint
1 tablespoon roughly
chopped cilantro
8–10 cherry tomatoes

SERVES 4–6

1 Heat the oil in a deep, round frying pan or a karahi. Lower the heat slightly, add the slit green chiles and fry until the skins start to change color. Remove the chiles to a plate.

2 Add the onion and cumin seeds, curry leaves, ginger, chili powder, ground cilantro, garlic, salt and onions to the pan and sauté for a few seconds, stirring the mixture constantly.

3 Add the chicken pieces and stir-fry for 7–10 minutes or until the chicken is cooked through.

4 Sprinkle the lemon juice on the chicken and add the mint and cilantro.

5 Add the cherry tomatoes and return the chiles to the pan. Heat through and serve with naan or parathas.

CHICKEN PASANDA

P asanda dishes are favorites in Pakistan, and now they are becoming so in the West.

INGREDIENTS
¼ cup plain yogurt
½ teaspoon black cumin seeds
4 cardamom pods
6 whole black peppercorns
2 teaspoons garam masala
1-inch piece cinnamon stick
1 tablespoon ground almonds
1 garlic clove, crushed
1 teaspoon sliced fresh ginger root
1 teaspoon chili powder
1 teaspoon salt
1½ pounds chicken, skinned, boned and cubed
5 tablespoons corn oil
2 onions, diced
3 fresh green chiles, chopped
2 tablespoons chopped cilantro
½ cup light cream

SERVES 4

1 Mix the yogurt, cumin seeds, cardamom pods, peppercorns, garam masala, cinnamon stick, ground almonds, garlic, ginger, chili powder and salt in a medium bowl. Add the chicken pieces, cover and let marinate for about 2 hours.

2 Heat the oil in a large karahi or deep, round frying pan. Add the onions and sauté for 2–3 minutes.

3 Add the chicken mixture and stir until it is thoroughly combined with the onions.

4 Cook the chicken and spice mixture over medium heat, stirring occasionally, for 12–15 minutes, or until the sauce is thickened and the chicken pieces are cooked through.

5 Add the green chiles and cilantro, pour in the cream and bring to a boil. Serve garnished with more cilantro, if desired.

CHICKEN WITH LENTILS

This recipe has a rather unusual combination of flavors, but it is well worth trying. The mango powder gives a delicious tangy flavor to the finished dish.

INGREDIENTS
½ cup chana dhal *(split yellow lentils)*
¼ cup corn oil
2 leeks, chopped
6 dried red chiles
4 curry leaves
1 teaspoon mustard seeds
2 teaspoons mango powder
2 tomatoes, chopped
½ teaspoon chili powder
1 teaspoon ground cilantro
1 teaspoon salt
1 pound chicken, skinned, boned and cubed
1 tablespoon chopped cilantro

SERVES 4–6

COOK'S TIP
Chana dhal is available at Asian specialty stores. However, split yellow peas from food stores and supermarkets make a good substitute.

1 Wash the lentils carefully under cold running water and remove any stones or pieces of grit.

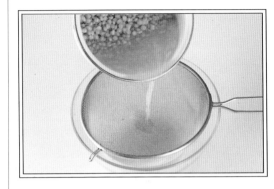

2 Put the lentils into a saucepan with enough water to cover and boil for about 10 minutes, until they are soft but not mushy. Drain and set aside in a bowl.

3 Heat the oil in a medium karahi or deep, round frying pan. Lower the heat slightly and add the leeks, dried red chiles, curry leaves and mustard seeds. Stir-fry gently for a few minutes.

4 Add the mango powder, tomatoes, chili powder, ground cilantro, salt and chicken and stir-fry for 7–10 minutes.

5 Mix in the cooked lentils and cook for another 2 minutes or until the chicken is thoroughly cooked.

6 Garnish with the cilantro and serve immediately.

POUSSINS IN TAMARIND SAUCE

The chiles make this a quite hot dish. Its subtle, sweet and sour flavor is due to the addition of the tamarind paste.

INGREDIENTS

¼ cup tomato ketchup

1 tablespoon tamarind paste

¼ cup water

1½ teaspoons chili powder

1½ teaspoons salt

1 tablespoon sugar

1½ teaspoons sliced fresh ginger root

1½ garlic cloves, crushed

2 tablespoons dry, shredded coconut

2 tablespoons sesame seeds

1 teaspoon poppy seeds

1 teaspoon ground cumin

1½ teaspoons ground cilantro

1 pound poussins, skinned and cut into 6–8 pieces each

5 tablespoons corn oil

8 curry leaves

½ teaspoon onion seeds

3 large dried red chiles

½ teaspoon fenugreek seeds

10–12 cherry tomatoes

3 tablespoons chopped cilantro

2 fresh green chiles, chopped

SERVES 4–6

1 Put the ketchup, tamarind paste and water a large bowl and blend together with a fork until they are thoroughly combined.

2 Add the chili powder, salt, sugar, ginger, garlic, coconut, sesame and poppy seeds, ground cumin and ground cilantro to the mixture.

3 Add the poussin pieces and stir until they are well coated with the spice mixture. Set aside.

4 Heat the oil in a deep, round frying pan or a large karahi. Add the curry leaves, onion seeds, red chiles and fenugreek seeds and fry for 1 minute.

5 Lower the heat to medium and add the poussin pieces with their sauce and stir well. Simmer for 12–15 minutes or until the poussin is thoroughly cooked.

6 Add the tomatoes, cilantro and green chiles, and serve with Colorful Pullao Rice, if desired.

CHICKEN BIRYANI

This is a classic Indian dish for important occasions and is truly fit for royalty. Serve it on a wide, shallow platter for maximum effect.

INGREDIENTS

3–3½ pounds skinless, boneless chicken
breast, cut into large pieces
¼ cup biryani masala paste
2 green chiles, chopped
1 tablespoon grated fresh ginger root
2 garlic cloves, crushed
2 ounces cilantro, chopped
6–8 fresh mint leaves, chopped
⅔ cup plain yogurt
4 onions, sliced, deep-fried and crushed
2½ cups basmati rice, washed
1 teaspoon black cumin seeds
2-inch piece cinnamon stick
6 green cardamom pods
vegetable oil, for shallow-frying
4 large potatoes, peeled and quartered
1¼ cups skim milk
few saffron threads, infused
in milk
salt
2 tablespoons ghee or unsalted butter,
plus extra for shallow-frying,
½ cup cashews and
⅓ cup golden raisins, to garnish

Serves 4–6

1 Mix the chicken with the next nine ingredients in a large bowl, cover and let marinate for about 2 hours. Place in a large heavy pan and cook gently for about 10 minutes. Set aside.

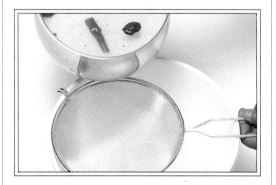

2 Boil a large pan of water. Add the rice with the cumin seeds, cinnamon stick and cardamom pods; soak for 5 minutes. Drain well. Remove the whole spices.

3 Heat the oil for shallow-frying and cook the potatoes until they are evenly browned on all sides. Drain and set aside.

4 Arrange half of the rice on top of the chicken pieces in the saucepan in an even layer, then make another even layer with the potatoes. Put the remaining rice on top of the potatoes and spread it out to make an even layer.

5 Sprinkle the skim milk all over the rice. Make random holes in the rice with the handle of a spoon and pour a little saffron-flavored milk into each one. Place a few knobs of ghee or butter on the surface of the rice, cover the pan tightly and cook over low heat for 35–45 minutes.

6 While the biryani is cooking, make the garnish. Heat a little ghee or butter and fry the cashews and golden raisins until they swell. Drain and set aside. When the biryani is ready, gently toss the rice, chicken and potatoes together. Transfer to a warmed serving platter, garnish with the nut and golden raisin mixture and serve immediately.

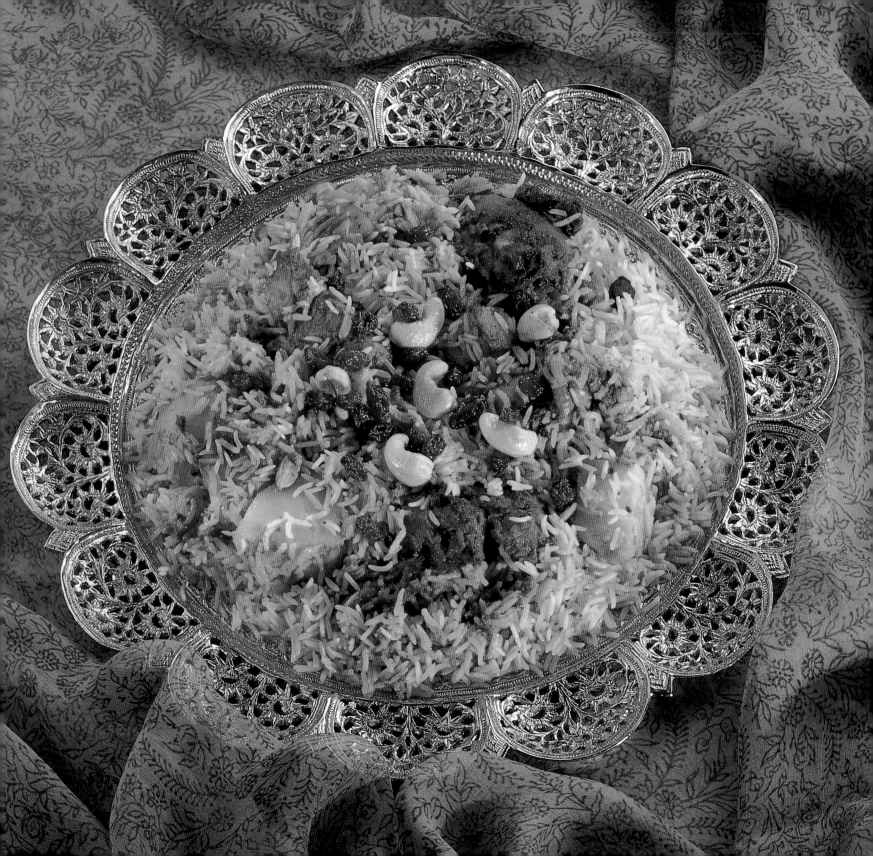

CHICKEN IN CASHEW SAUCE

This chicken dish has a deliciously thick and nutty sauce, and is best served with plain boiled rice. Cashews grow profusely in southern India and are widely used in cooking.

INGREDIENTS
2 onions

2 tablespoons tomato paste

½ cup cashews

1½ teaspoons garam masala

1 garlic clove, crushed

1 teaspoon chili powder

1 tablespoon lemon juice

¼ teaspoon ground turmeric

1 teaspoon salt

1 tablespoon plain yogurt

2 tablespoons corn oil

1 tablespoon chopped cilantro

1 tablespoon golden raisins

1 pound skinless, boneless chicken breasts, cut into pieces

6 ounces button mushrooms

1¼ cups water

1 tablespoon chopped cilantro, to garnish

SERVES 4

1 Cut the onions into quarters and place in a food processor or blender. Process for about 1 minute.

2 Add the tomato paste, cashews, garam masala, garlic, chili powder, lemon juice, turmeric, salt and yogurt and process for another 1–1½ minutes.

3 Heat the oil in a saucepan and pour in the spice mixture. Fry for 2 minutes, over medium to low heat. Add the cilantro, golden raisins and chicken, and stir-fry the mixture for 1 minute.

4 Add the mushrooms, pour in the water and bring to a simmer. Cover the saucepan and cook over low heat for about 10 minutes. Check that the chicken is cooked through and the sauce is thick. Cook for a little longer, if necessary.

5 To serve, ladle the chicken and its sauce onto a warmed serving dish. Garnish with the chopped cilantro.

GRILLED CHICKEN

Grilled chicken is served almost everywhere in Thailand, from portable roadside stalls to sports stadiums and beaches. For an authentic touch, serve with rice on a banana leaf.

INGREDIENTS
1 chicken, 3–3½-pound,
cut into 8–10 pieces
2 limes, cut into wedges,
2 red chiles, finely sliced, and
a few lemongrass stalks, to garnish

FOR THE MARINADE
2 lemongrass stalks, chopped
1-inch piece fresh ginger root
6 garlic cloves
4 shallots
½ bunch cilantro roots
1 tablespoon dark brown sugar
½ cup coconut milk
2 tablespoons fish sauce
2 tablespoons soy sauce

SERVES 4–6

1 To make the marinade, put all the ingredients into a food processor and process until smooth.

2 Put the chicken pieces in a dish and pour in the marinade. Set in a cool place to marinate for at least 4 hours or preferably overnight.

3 Grill the chicken over glowing coals, or place it on a rack over a baking sheet and bake at 400°F for 20–30 minutes or until the chicken is cooked and golden brown. Turn the pieces occasionally and brush with the marinade.

4 Garnish with lime wedges, finely sliced red chiles and lemongrass.

STIR-FRIED CHICKEN WITH BASIL AND CHILES

T his quick and easy chicken dish is an excellent introduction to Thai cuisine. Deep-frying the basil adds another dimension to this recipe. Thai basil, also known as holy basil, has a unique, pungent flavor that is both spicy and sharp. The dull-colored leaves have serrated edges.

INGREDIENTS
3 tablespoons vegetable oil
4 garlic cloves, sliced
2–4 red chiles, seeded and chopped
1 pound chicken, cut into
bite-size pieces
2–3 tablespoons fish sauce
2 teaspoons dark soy sauce
1 teaspoon sugar
10–12 Thai basil leaves
2 red chiles, finely sliced, and
20 Thai basil leaves, deep-fried
(optional), to garnish

SERVES 4–6

COOK'S TIP
To deep-fry Thai basil leaves, make sure that the leaves are completely dry. Deep-fry in hot oil for 30–40 seconds, lift out and drain on paper towels.

1 Heat the oil in a wok or large frying pan and swirl it around.

2 Add the garlic and chiles and stir-fry until golden.

3 Add the chicken and stir-fry until it changes color.

4 Season with fish sauce, soy sauce and sugar. Continue to stir-fry for another 3–4 minutes or until the chicken is cooked through. Stir in the fresh Thai basil leaves. Garnish with sliced red chiles and the deep-fried basil, if using.

RED CHICKEN CURRY WITH BAMBOO SHOOTS

amboo shoots lend a crunchy texture to this classic Thai dish.

INGREDIENTS
4 cups coconut milk
1 pound diced boneless chicken
2 tablespoons fish sauce
1 tablespoon sugar
8 ounces bamboo shoots, sliced
5 kaffir lime leaves, torn
salt and freshly ground black pepper
chiles, basil and mint leaves, to garnish

FOR THE RED CURRY PASTE
12–15 red chiles, seeded
4 shallots, thinly sliced
2 garlic cloves, chopped
1 tablespoon chopped galangal
2 stalks lemongrass, chopped
3 kaffir lime leaves, chopped
4 cilantro roots
10 black peppercorns
1 teaspoon cilantro seeds
1/2 teaspoon cumin seeds
good pinch of ground cinnamon
1 teaspoon ground turmeric
1/2 teaspoon shrimp paste
1 teaspoon salt
2 tablespoons oil

SERVES 4–6

1 For the red curry paste, combine the all the ingredients in a mortar and pestle except for the oil, and pound until smooth.

2 Add the oil a little at a time and blend in well. Place in a jar in the refrigerator until ready to use. It will keep for 2 weeks.

3 In a large heavy saucepan, bring half the coconut milk to a boil, stirring until it separates.

4 Add 2 tablespoons red curry paste and cook for a few minutes.

5 Add the chicken, fish sauce and sugar. Fry for 3–5 minutes, until the chicken changes color, stirring constantly to prevent it from sticking to the pan.

6 Add the rest of the coconut milk, bamboo shoots and lime leaves. Return to a boil. Season to taste. Serve garnished with chiles, basil and mint leaves.

COOK'S TIP
It is quite acceptable to use canned bamboo, if fresh bamboo is not available. Whenever possible, buy whole canned bamboo, as it is generally crisper and of better quality than sliced shoots.

TANGY CHICKEN SALAD

his fresh and lively dish typifies the character of Thai cuisine. It is ideal for an appetizer or light lunch.

INGREDIENTS

4 skinned, boneless chicken breasts
2 garlic cloves, crushed and
roughly chopped
2 tablespoons soy sauce
2 tablespoons vegetable oil
½ cup coconut milk
2 tablespoons fish sauce
juice of 1 lime
2 tablespoons sugar
4 ounces water chestnuts, sliced
2 ounces cashews, roasted
4 shallots, finely sliced
4 kaffir lime leaves, finely sliced
1 lemongrass stalk, finely sliced
1 teaspoon chopped galangal
1 large red chile, seeded and
finely sliced
2 scallions, finely sliced
10–12 mint leaves, torn
1 head of lettuce, to serve
sprigs of cilantro and 2 red chiles, seeded
and sliced, to garnish

SERVES 4–6

1 Trim the chicken breasts of any excess fat and put them in a large dish. Rub with the garlic, soy sauce and 1 tablespoon of the oil. Let marinate for 1–2 hours.

2 Broil or pan-fry the chicken for 3–4 minutes on both sides or until cooked. Remove and set aside to cool.

3 In a small saucepan, heat the coconut milk, fish sauce, lime juice and sugar. Stir until all of the sugar has dissolved ,and then remove from heat.

4 Cut the cooked chicken into strips and combine with the water chestnuts, cashews, shallots, kaffir lime leaves, lemongrass, galangal, red chile, scallions and mint leaves.

5 Pour the coconut dressing onto the chicken, toss and mix well. Serve the chicken on a bed of lettuce leaves and garnish with sprigs of cilantro and sliced red chiles.

CHIANG MAI SALAD

Chiang Mai is a city in the northeast of Thailand. The city is culturally very close to Laos and famous for its chicken salad, which was originally called "Laap" or "Larp." Duck, beef or pork can be used instead of chicken.

INGREDIENTS
1 pound ground chicken
1 lemongrass stalk, finely chopped
3 kaffir lime leaves, finely chopped
4 red chiles, seeded and chopped
¼ cup lime juice
2 tablespoons fish sauce
1 tablespoon roasted ground rice
2 scallions, chopped
2 tablespoons cilantro leaves
mixed salad greens, to serve
cucumber and tomato slices, and a few sprigs of mint, to garnish

SERVES 4–6

1 Heat a large non stick frying pan. Add the ground chicken and a little water to moisten while cooking.

2 Stir constantly until cooked; this will take 7–10 minutes.

3 Transfer the cooked chicken to a large bowl and add the rest of the ingredients. Mix thoroughly.

4 Serve on a bed of mixed salad greens and garnish with cucumber, tomato slices and a few sprigs of mint.

COOK'S TIP
Use sticky, or glutinous, rice to make roasted ground rice. Put the rice in a frying pan and dry-roast until golden brown. Remove and grind to a powder in a mortar and pestle or in a food processor. Keep in a glass jar in a cool and dry place and use as needed.

HOT-AND-SOUR CHICKEN SALAD

 delicious substantial salad from Vietnam, known as *Nuong Ngu Vi*, with a piquant peanut flavor.

INGREDIENTS
2 chicken breast fillets, skinned
1 small red chile, seeded and finely chopped
1 piece fresh ginger root, ½ inch long, peeled and finely chopped
1 clove garlic, crushed
1 tablespoon crunchy peanut butter
2 tablespoons chopped cilantro leaves
1 teaspoon sugar
½ teaspoon salt
1 tablespoon rice or white wine vinegar
¼ cup vegetable oil
2 teaspoons fish sauce (optional)

FOR THE SALAD
4 ounces bean sprouts
1 head Chinese greens, roughly shredded
2 medium carrots, cut into thin sticks
1 red onion, cut into fine rings
2 large gherkins, sliced

SERVES 4–6

1 Slice the chicken thinly, place in a shallow bowl and set aside. Grind the chile, ginger and garlic in a mortar and pestle. Transfer to a small bowl and add the peanut butter, cilantro leaves, sugar and salt. Mix thoroughly.

2 Add the vinegar, 2 tablespoons of the oil and the fish sauce, if using, to the small bowl. Combine well. Brush this spice mixture all over the chicken strips and let marinate in a cool place for at least 2–3 hours, until the flavors have soaked into the meat.

3 Heat the remaining 2 tablespoons of oil in a wok or deep frying pan. Add the chicken to the hot oil and cook for 10–12 minutes, tossing the meat occasionally. Serve hot, with the salad.

BALINESE SPICED DUCK

D uck is a popular ingredient all over Asia. Cooked Balinese-style, in coconut milk and spices, it is deliciously moist and tender.

INGREDIENTS
8 duck pieces, fat trimmed and reserved
1/4 cup dry, shredded coconut
3/4 cup coconut milk
salt and freshly ground black pepper
deep-fried onions, to garnish
salad and chopped herbs, to serve

FOR THE SPICE PASTE
1 small onion or 4–6 shallots, sliced
2 garlic cloves, sliced
1/2-inch piece fresh ginger root,
peeled and sliced
1/2-inch piece fresh lengkuas,
peeled and sliced
1-inch piece fresh turmeric or 1/2 teaspoon
ground turmeric
1–2 red chiles, seeded and sliced
4 macadamia nuts or 8 almonds
1 teaspoon coriander seeds, dry-fried

SERVES 4

1 Place the duck fat trimmings in a heated frying pan, without oil, and let the fat drip off. Reserve the fat.

2 Fry the coconut in a preheated pan without oil, until crisp and brown in color.

3 To make the spice paste, blend the onion or shallots, garlic, ginger, *lengkuas*, fresh or ground turmeric, chiles, nuts and cilantro seeds into a paste in a food processor or with a mortar and pestle.

4 Spread half the spice paste on the duck portions and let marinate in a cool place for 3–4 hours. Preheat the oven to 325°F. Transfer the duck breasts to an oiled roasting pan. Cover with a double layer of aluminum foil and cook the duck for about 2 hours. When cooked, remove the duck from the pan and set aside to keep warm. Reserve the fat and juices from the duck and keep in the pan.

5 Turn the oven temperature up to 375°F. Heat the reserved duck fat in a pan, add the remaining spice paste and fry for 1–2 minutes. Stir in the coconut milk and simmer for 2 minutes. Cover the duck with the spice mixture and sprinkle with the fried coconut. Cook for 20–30 minutes.

6 Arrange the duck on a platter and garnish with deep-fried onions. Season to taste and serve with the salad and herbs.

CRISPY AROMATIC DUCK

Because this dish is often served with pancakes, scallions, cucumber and duck sauce or plum sauce, many people mistakenly think it is Peking duck. This recipe, however, uses quite a different cooking method. The result is just as crispy, but the delightful aroma makes this dish particularly distinctive. Thin pancakes are widely available at Chinese supermarkets.

INGREDIENTS

1 oven-ready duckling,
weighing 4½–5 pounds
2 teaspoons salt
5–6 whole star anise
1 tablespoon Szechuan peppercorns
1 teaspoon cloves
2–3 cinnamon sticks
3–4 scallions
3–4 slices fresh ginger root, unpeeled
5–6 tablespoons Chinese rice wine or
dry sherry
vegetable oil, for deep-frying
lettuce leaves, to garnish
12–16 thin pancakes, plum sauce,
½ bunch shredded scallions,
½ cucumber cut into matchstick
strips, to serve

SERVES 6–8

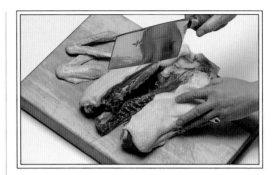

1 Remove the wings from the duck. Split the body in half down the backbone. Rub salt all over the two duck halves, taking care to rub it in. Place the duck in a dish with the spices, the scallions, ginger and rice wine or sherry. Let the duck marinate for at least 4–6 hours, turning occasionally.

2 Steam the duck vigorously with the marinade for 3–4 hours (longer if possible), then remove from the cooking liquid and let cool, covered, for at least 5–6 hours. The duck must be completely cold and dry, or the skin will not be crispy.

3 Heat the oil in a wok until smoking, place the duck pieces in the oil, skin-side down, and deep-fry for 5–6 minutes or until crisp and brown, turning just once at the very last moment.

4 Remove the duck from the wok with a slotted spoon and drain on paper towels. Arrange the lettuce leaves on a large platter. To serve, place the duck on the lettuce and remove from the bone at the table or before serving. Each guest places a few pieces of meat on a pancake, adds some sauce, scallion and cucumber, then rolls up the pancake.

STIR-FRIED TURKEY WITH SNOWPEAS

The crunchiness of the snowpeas, water chestnuts, scallions and cashews gives this Chinese turkey dish an interesting texture.

INGREDIENTS

2 tablespoons sesame oil
6 tablespoons lemon juice
1 garlic clove, crushed
½-inch piece fresh ginger root, peeled and grated
1 teaspoon honey
1 pound turkey fillets, cut into strips
4 ounces snowpeas, trimmed
2 tablespoons peanut oil
½ cup cashews
6 scallions, cut into strips
8-ounce can water chestnuts, drained and thinly sliced
salt
saffron rice, to serve

SERVES 4

1 Combine the sesame oil, lemon juice, garlic, ginger and honey in a shallow nonmetallic dish. Add the turkey and mix well. Cover and let marinate for 3–4 hours, stirring occasionally.

2 Blanch the snowpeas in boiling salted water for 1 minute. Drain and refresh under cold running water.

3 Drain the marinade from the turkey strips and reserve the marinade. Heat the peanut oil in a wok or large frying pan, add the cashews and stir-fry for 1–2 minutes until golden brown. Using a slotted spoon, remove the cashews from the wok and set them aside.

4 Add the turkey strips to the wok and stir-fry for 3–4 minutes, until they are golden brown on all sides. Add the scallions, snowpeas and water chestnuts and pour in the reserved marinade. Cook for a few minutes, until the turkey is tender and the sauce is bubbling and hot.

5 Return the nuts to the wok and stir in. Transfer to a warmed serving platter and serve immediately, with saffron rice.

CHICKEN AND VEGETABLE STIR-FRY

Make this quick supper dish a little hotter and spicier by adding either more fresh ginger root or oyster sauce, if desired.

INGREDIENTS
zest of ½ lemon
½-inch piece fresh ginger root
1 large garlic clove
2 tablespoons sunflower oil
10 ounces lean chicken, thinly sliced
½ red bell pepper, seeded and sliced
½ green bell pepper, seeded and sliced
4 scallions, chopped
2 carrots, cut into matchsticks
4 ounces fine green beans
2 tablespoons oyster sauce
pinch of sugar
¼ cup salted peanuts,
lightly crushed
salt and ground black pepper
cilantro leaves, to garnish
rice, to serve

SERVES 4

1 Thinly slice the lemon zest. Peel and chop the ginger and garlic. Heat the oil in a frying pan or wok over high heat. Add the lemon zest, ginger and garlic, and stir- fry for 30 seconds, until brown.

2 Add the chicken and stir-fry for 2 minutes. Add the vegetables *(left)* and stir-fry for 4–5 minutes, until the chicken is cooked and the vegetables are tender.

3 Finally, stir in the oyster sauce, sugar, peanuts and seasoning to taste and stir-fry for another minute to mix and blend well. Serve immediately, sprinkled with the cilantro leaves and accompanied by rice.

CHICKEN WITH CHINESE VEGETABLES

The chicken in this recipe can be replaced by almost any other meat, such as pork, beef or liver—or you can even use shrimp, if desired.

INGREDIENTS

8–10 ounces chicken, boned and skinned
1 teaspoon salt
½ egg white, lightly beaten
2 teaspoons cornstarch, mixed with a little water
¼ cup vegetable oil
6–8 small dried shiitake mushrooms, soaked
4 ounces sliced bamboo shoots, drained
4 ounces snowpeas, trimmed
1 scallion, cut into short sections
a few small pieces fresh root ginger root, peeled
1 teaspoon light brown sugar
1 tablespoon light soy sauce
1 tablespoon Chinese rice wine or dry sherry
few drops of sesame oil, to serve

SERVES 4

1 Cut the chicken into thin 1-inch slices. In a bowl, mix a pinch of the salt with the egg white and cornstarch paste.

2 Heat a wok, then add the oil. When it is hot, add the chicken slices and stir-fry over medium heat for about 30 seconds, then, using a slotted spoon, transfer to a plate and keep warm.

3 Add the mushrooms, bamboo shoots, snowpeas, scallion and ginger and stir-fry over high heat for about 1 minute. Add the salt, sugar, and chicken. Blend together, then add the soy sauce and wine or sherry. Stir a few more times, then sprinkle with the sesame oil and serve.

SZECHUAN-STYLE KUNG PO CHICKEN

Kung Po was the name of a court official in Szechuan; his cook created this dish. Omit some or all of the chiles for a less spicy dish.

INGREDIENTS

12 ounces chicken thighs, skinned and boned
¼ teaspoon salt
½ egg white, lightly beaten
2 teaspoons cornstarch, mixed with water
1 green bell pepper, cored and seeded
¼ cup vegetable oil
3–4 whole dried red chiles, soaked in water for 10 minutes
1 scallion, cut into short sections
few small pieces fresh ginger root, peeled
1 tablespoon sweet bean paste or hoi sin sauce
1 teaspoon hot bean paste
1 tablespoon Chinese rice wine or dry sherry
1 cup roasted cashews and a few drops of sesame oil, to serve

SERVES 4

1 Cut the chicken into ½-inch cubes. In a bowl, mix the chicken with the salt, egg white and cornstarch paste. Cut the green pepper into squares about the same size as the chicken cubes.

2 Heat a wok, then add the oil. When it is hot, add the chicken cubes and stir-fry for about 1 minute or until the color changes. Remove the chicken from the wok with a slotted spoon and keep warm.

3 Add the green pepper, soaked red chiles, scallion and ginger and stir-fry for about 1 minute.

4 Add the chicken to the wok with the sweet bean paste or hoisin sauce, hot bean paste and wine or sherry. Blend thoroughly and cook for another minute. Finally stir in the cashews and sesame oil. Transfer to a warmed serving platter and serve immediately.

SOY-BRAISED CHICKEN

This dish can be served hot or cold. Soy sauce is a vital ingredient in Chinese cooking. Light soy sauce is thinner and saltier than dark.

INGREDIENTS

1 whole chicken, weighing 3–3½ pounds
1 tablespoon ground Szechuan peppercorns
2 tablespoons finely chopped fresh ginger root
3 tablespoons light soy sauce
2 tablespoons dark soy sauce
3 tablespoons Chinese rice wine or sherry
1 tablespoon light brown sugar
vegetable oil, for deep-frying
2½ cups chicken stock or water
2 teaspoons salt
2 tablespoons sugar
lettuce leaves, to garnish

SERVES 6–8
AS PART OF A LARGER MEAL

1 Rub the chicken, both inside and out, with the Szechuan pepper and ginger. Marinate the bird with the soy sauces, wine or sherry and sugar for 3 hours, turning the bird several times.

2 Heat a wok, then add the oil. When it is hot, add the chicken, reserving the marinade, and deep-fry for 5–6 minutes or until brown all over.

3 Remove and drain. Pour off the excess oil, add the marinade with the stock or water, salt and the sugar and bring to a boil. Return the chicken to the wok and braise in the sauce, covered, for 35–40 minutes, turning once or twice.

4 Remove the chicken and let it cool a little before chopping it into about 30 bite-size pieces. Arrange the chicken pieces on a bed of lettuce leaves, then pour on some of the sauce and serve immediately. Use the remaining sauce another time.

MEAT DISHES

Spices have the dual effect of flavoring and tenderizing meat. This makes Indian dishes such as Lentils with Lamb and Tomatoes tender to the taste and redolent with the flavors of turmeric, chile, cinnamon and cilantro.

Until quite recently, meat did not play a large part in Asian cuisines, in part for religious or legal reasons and because land was scarce there were few places to graze livestock.

Today meat is one of many ingredients in a dish rather than being the sole ingredient. In Chinese and Japanese dishes the meat is cooked simply and for the minimum of time, requiring good quality, lean cuts of meat. The flavors of orange, ginger, soy sauce, mooli and dashi or Szechuan peppercorns augment the taste.

Meat curries, by contrast, combine numerous ingredients with rich sauces. Mussaman Curry from Thailand uses a curry paste of that name full of chile, garlic, galangal, lemongrass, and various seeds and spices. The paste can be stored for four months and used with this dish, which features steak, potatoes, peanuts and coconut, or with other ingredients of your choice.

LAMB WITH SPINACH

L amb with Spinach is a well-known recipe from the Punjab region. It is important to use red bell peppers, as they add such a distinctive flavor to the finished dish.

INGREDIENTS

1 teaspoon sliced fresh ginger root
1 garlic clove, crushed
1½ teaspoons chili powder
1 teaspoon salt
1 teaspoon garam masala
6 tablespoons corn oil
2 onions, sliced
1½ pounds lean lamb, cut into
2-inch cubes
2½–3¾ cups water
14 ounces fresh spinach
1 large red bell pepper, seeded and chopped
3 fresh green chiles, chopped
3 tablespoons chopped cilantro
1 tablespoon lemon juice (optional)

SERVES 4–6

COOK'S TIP
Frozen spinach can also be used for this dish, but try to find whole leaf spinach rather than the chopped kind—it has a much better flavor.

---

1 Combine the ginger, garlic, chili powder, salt and garam masala in a bowl. Set aside.

2 Heat the oil in a saucepan, add the onions and sauté for 10–12 minutes or until well browned. Add the lamb pieces and stir-fry for about 2 minutes.

3 Add the spice mixture and stir thoroughly until the lamb is well coated. Pour in the water and bring to a boil, then cover the pan and lower the heat. Cook gently for 25–35 minutes without letting the contents of the pan burn. If there is still a lot of water remaining in the pan, remove the lid and boil briskly to evaporate the excess.

4 Meanwhile, wash and roughly chop the spinach, discarding any tough stalks, then blanch it for about 1 minute in a pan of boiling water. Drain well.

5 Add the spinach to the lamb and cook for 7–10 minutes, using a wooden spoon in a semi-circular motion, scraping the bottom of the pan as you stir.

6 Add the red pepper, green chiles and chopped cilantro to the pan and stir over medium heat for 2 minutes. Sprinkle with the lemon juice, if using, and serve immediately. Serve with a simple accompaniment such as plain boiled rice or naan.

KHARA MASALA LAMB

Whole spices (*khara*) are used in this curry, so you should warn your guests. It is delicious with freshly baked naan or boiled rice.

INGREDIENTS
5 tablespoons corn oil
2 onions, chopped
1 teaspoon sliced fresh ginger root
1 garlic clove, sliced
6 dried red chiles
3 cardamom pods
2 cinnamon sticks
6 black peppercorns
3 cloves
½ teaspoon salt
1-pound boned leg of lamb, cubed
2½ cups water
2 fresh green chiles, sliced
2 tablespoons chopped cilantro

SERVES 4

COOK'S TIP
The technique of stirring the meat and spices with a semi-circular motion, used in step 3, is called *bhoonoing*. It ensures that the meat is well coated with the spice mixture before the cooking liquid is added.

1 Heat the oil in a large saucepan, lower the heat slightly, add the onions, and sauté until they are lightly browned.

2 Add half of the ginger and half of the garlic and stir well. Add half of the red chiles, the cardamom pods, cinnamon, peppercorns, cloves and salt.

3 Add the lamb and fry over medium heat. Stir constantly for 5 minutes with a semi-circular movement, using a wooden spoon to scrape the bottom of the pan.

4 Pour in the water, cover with a lid and cook over medium low heat for 35–40 minutes or until the water has evaporated and the meat is tender.

5 Add the remaining ginger, garlic and dried red chiles to the pan, then stir in the fresh green chiles and the chopped cilantro.

6 Continue cooking, stirring constantly, until you see some free oil on the sides of the pan. Transfer to a warmed serving dish and serve immediately.

LAMB-STUFFED VEGETABLES

ggplant and bell peppers make a good combination. Here they are stuffed with an aromatic lamb filling.

INGREDIENTS
3 small eggplant
1 each red, green and yellow bell pepper

FOR THE STUFFING
3 tablespoons corn oil
3 onions, sliced
1 teaspoon chili powder
¼ teaspoon turmeric
1 teaspoon ground cilantro
1 teaspoon ground cumin
1 garlic clove, crushed
1 teaspoon salt
1 pound lean ground lamb
2 tablespoons chopped cilantro

FOR THE SAUTEED ONIONS
3 tablespoons corn oil
1 teaspoon mixed onion, mustard, fenugreek and white cumin seeds
4 dried red chiles
3 onions, roughly chopped
1 teaspoon salt
2 tomatoes, sliced
2 fresh green chiles, chopped
2 tablespoons chopped cilantro

SERVES 6

1 Prepare the vegetables. Slit the eggplant lengthwise up to the stems, leaving the stems intact. Cut the tops off the peppers and scoop out the seeds. You can keep the pepper tops to use as "lids" for the stuffed vegetables, if desired.

2 To make the stuffing, heat the oil in a saucepan. Add the onions and sauté for about 3 minutes. Lower the heat and add the chili powder, turmeric, ground cilantro, ground cumin, garlic and salt, and stir-fry for about 1 ground. Add the ground lamb and turn up the heat.

3 Stir-fry for 7–10 minutes, or until the lamb is cooked. Add the cilantro toward the end of the cooking time and stir to mix. Remove the lamb mixture from heat, cover and set aside.

4 Make the sautéed onions. Heat the oil in a deep, round frying pan or a karahi and add the mixed onion, mustard, fenugreek and white cumin seeds and red chiles and cook for another. Add the onions and cook for 2 minutes or until soft.

5 Add the salt, sliced tomatoes, chopped green chiles and the chopped cilantro and cook for 1 further minute. Remove from heat and set aside.

6 When the ground lamb mixture is cool, stuff the eggplant and peppers. Using a small spoon, fill them quite loosely with the lamb mixture.

7 Place the stuffed vegetables on top of the sautéed onions in the karahi. Cover with aluminum foil, making sure the foil doesn't touch the food, and cook over low heat for about 15 minutes, until the eggplant and peppers are tender. Serve with a dish of plain boiled rice or Colorful Pullao Rice.

COOK'S TIP
Large beef tomatoes are also delicious stuffed with this lightly spiced lamb mixture. Simply cut off the tops and scoop out the cores, seeds and some of the pulp and cook as above.

LENTILS WITH LAMB AND TOMATOES

This aromatically spiced dish is rich in protein and has a deliciously light texture. Colorful Pullao Rice makes a perfect accompaniment.

INGREDIENTS

¼ cup corn oil

2 bay leaves

2 cloves

4 black peppercorns

1 onion, sliced

1 pound lean lamb, boned and cubed

¼ teaspoon ground turmeric

1½ teaspoons chili powder

1 teaspoon crushed cilantro seeds

1-inch piece cinnamon stick

1 garlic clove, crushed

1½ teaspoons salt

6¼ cups water

⅓ cup chana dhal *(split yellow lentils) or yellow split peas*

2 tomatoes, quartered

2 fresh green chiles, chopped

1 tablespoon chopped cilantro

SERVES 4

1 Heat the oil in a deep, round frying pan or a karahi. Lower the heat slightly and add the bay leaves, cloves, peppercorns and onion and sauté for about 5 minutes or until the onions are golden.

2 Add the lamb cubes, ground turmeric, chili powder, cilantro seeds, cinnamon stick, garlic and most of the salt to the pan. Stir-fry the lamb mixture for about 5 minutes over medium heat.

3 Pour in 3¾ cups of the water and cover the pan with a lid or aluminum foil, making sure the foil does not come into contact with the contents of the pan. Simmer the lamb over low heat for 35–40 minutes, or until the water has evaporated and the lamb is tender.

4 Meanwhile, put the lentils into a saucepan with the remaining 2½ cups water and boil for 12–15 minutes or until the water has almost evaporated and the lentils are soft enough to mash easily. If the lentil mixture is too thick, gradually add up to ⅔ cup water until they mash easily.

5 When the lamb is tender, stir-fry the mixture using a wooden spoon, until some free oil begins to appear on the sides of the pan.

6 Add the cooked lentils to the lamb and combine well with a wooden spoon.

7 Stir in the tomatoes, chiles and cilantro, then transfer to a warmed serving dish and serve immediately.

VARIATION

Boned and cubed chicken can be used in place of the lamb. At step 3, reduce the amount of water to 1¼ cups and cook uncovered, stirring occasionally, for 10–15 minutes or until the water has evaporated and the chicken is cooked through.

MUSSAMAN CURRY

This curry is Indian in origin. Traditionally it is made with beef, but chicken or lamb can be used, or you can make a vegetarian version using tofu. It has a rich, sweet and spicy flavor. Serve with boiled rice.

INGREDIENTS
3½ cups coconut milk
1½ pounds stewing beef, cut into
1-inch chunks
3 tablespoons Mussaman curry paste
(see Cook's Tip)
2 tablespoons fish sauce
1 tablespoon sugar
¼ cup tamarind juice
6 cardamom pods
1 cinnamon stick
8 ounces potatoes, cut into
even-size chunks
1 onion, cut into wedges
2 ounces roasted peanuts
boiled rice, to serve

SERVES 4–6

1 Bring 2½ cups of the coconut milk to a gentle boil in a large saucepan. Add the beef and simmer for about 40 minutes, until tender.

2 Put the the rest of the coconut milk into a saucepan, then cook for 5–8 minutes, stirring constantly.

3 Add the Mussaman curry paste and fry until fragrant. Add the fried curry paste to the pan containing the cooked beef.

4 Add the fish sauce, sugar, tamarind juice, cardamom pods, cinnamon stick, potato chunks and onion. Simmer until the potatoes are cooked, for 10–15 minutes.

5 Add the roasted peanuts. Cook for another 5 minutes, then serve with rice.

COOK'S TIP
Mussaman curry paste is used to make the Thai version of a Muslim curry. It can be prepared and then stored in a glass jar in the refrigerator for up to four months.
Remove the seeds from 12 large dried chiles and soak in hot water for 15 minutes. Combine ¼ cup chopped shallots, 5 garlic cloves, 1 chopped lemongrass stalk, 2 teaspoons chopped galangal, 1 teaspoon cumin seeds, 1 tablespoon cilantro seeds, 2 cloves and 6 black peppercorns. Place in a wok and dry-fry over low heat for 5–6 minutes. Grind or process into a powder and stir in 1 teaspoon shrimp paste, 1 teaspoon salt, 1 teaspoon sugar and 2 tablespoons oil.

FRAGRANT THAI MEATBALLS

A creamy peanut sauce accompanies these tasty little meatballs, which can be made of beef or pork.

INGREDIENTS
1 pound lean ground pork or beef
1 tablespoon chopped garlic
1 lemongrass stalk, finely chopped
4 scallions, finely chopped
1 tablespoon chopped cilantro
2 tablespoons red curry paste
1 tablespoon lemon juice
1 tablespoon fish sauce
1 egg
salt and freshly ground black pepper
rice flour, for dusting
oil, for deep-frying
sprigs of cilantro, to garnish

FOR THE PEANUT SAUCE
1 tablespoon vegetable oil
1 tablespoon red curry paste
2 tablespoons crunchy peanut butter
1 tablespoon sugar
1 tablespoon lemon juice
1 cup coconut milk

SERVES 4–6

1 Make the peanut sauce. Heat the oil in a small saucepan, add the curry paste and fry for 1 minute.

2 Stir in the rest of the sauce ingredients and bring to a boil. Lower the heat and simmer for 5 minutes, until the sauce has thickened.

3 Make the meatballs. Combine all the ingredients except for the rice flour, oil and cilantro, and add some seasoning. Combine everything well.

4 Roll and shape the meat into small balls about the size of a walnut. Dust the meatballs with rice flour.

5 Heat the oil in a wok until hot and deep-fry the meatballs in batches until nicely browned and cooked through. Drain them on paper towels. Serve garnished with sprigs of cilantro and accompanied by the peanut sauce.

STIR-FRIED BEEF IN OYSTER SAUCE

Another simple but delicious recipe. In Thailand fresh straw mushrooms are readily available, but oyster mushrooms make a good substitute. To make the dish even more interesting, use several types of mushroom.

INGREDIENTS
1 pound rump steak
2 tablespoons soy sauce
1 tablespoon cornstarch
3 tablespoons vegetable oil
1 tablespoon chopped garlic
1 tablespoon chopped ginger root
8 ounces mixed mushrooms, such as
shiitake, oyster and straw
2 tablespoons oyster sauce
1 teaspoon sugar
4 scallions, cut into short lengths
freshly ground black pepper
2 red chiles, cut into strips, to garnish

SERVES 4–6

COOK'S TIP
Made from extracts of oysters, oyster sauce is velvety smooth and has a savory-sweet and meaty taste. There are several types available; buy the best you can afford.

1 Slice the beef, on the diagonal, into long thin strips. Combine the soy sauce and cornstarch in a large bowl, stir in the beef and let marinate for 1–2 hours.

2 Heat half the oil in a wok or frying pan. Add the garlic and ginger and cook until fragrant. Stir in the strips of beef. Stir to separate the pieces, let them color and cook for 1–2 minutes. Remove from the pan and set aside.

3 Heat the remaining oil in the wok. Add your selection of mushrooms, and cook until tender.

4 Return the beef to the wok with the mushrooms. Add the oyster sauce, sugar and freshly ground black pepper to taste. Mix well.

5 Add the scallions. Combine. Serve garnished with strips of red chile.

GREEN BEEF CURRY WITH THAI EGGPLANT

his is a very quick curry to make, so be sure to use tender, good-quality meat.

INGREDIENTS
3 tablespoons vegetable oil
2½ cups coconut milk
1 pound beef sirloin
4 kaffir lime leaves, torn
1–2 tablespoons fish sauce
1 teaspoon palm sugar
5 ounces small Thai eggplant, halved
a small handful of Thai basil
2 green chiles, shredded to garnish

FOR THE GREEN CURRY PASTE
15 hot green chiles
2 lemongrass stalks, chopped
3 shallots, sliced
2 garlic cloves
1 tablespoon chopped galangal
4 kaffir lime leaves, chopped
½ teaspoon grated kaffir lime zest
1 teaspoon chopped cilantro root
6 black peppercorns
1 teaspoon cilantro seeds, roasted
1 teaspoon cumin seeds, roasted
1 tablespoon sugar
1 teaspoon salt
1 teaspoon shrimp paste (optional)

SERVES 4–6

1 Make the green curry paste. Combine all the ingredients together thoroughly. Pound them in a mortar and pestle or process in a food processor until smooth. Add 2 tablespoons of the oil, a little at a time, and blend well between each addition. Keep in a glass jar in the refrigerator until needed.

2 Heat the remaining oil in a large saucepan or wok. Add 3 tablespoons green curry paste and fry until fragrant.

3 Stir in half the coconut milk, a little at a time. Cook for 5–6 minutes, until an oily sheen appears.

4 Cut the beef into long thin slices and add to the saucepan with the kaffir lime leaves, fish sauce, sugar and eggplant. Cook for 2–3 minutes, then stir in the remaining coconut milk.

5 Bring back to a simmer and cook until the meat and eggplant are tender. Stir in the Thai basil just before serving. Garnish with the shredded green chiles.

THAI BEEF SALAD

 hearty salad of beef, laced with a chile and lime dressing that perfectly complements the meat.

INGREDIENTS

8 ounces sirloin steaks
1 red onion, finely sliced
½ cucumber, cut into thin ribbons
1 lemongrass stalk, finely chopped
2 tablespoons chopped scallions
juice of 2 limes
1–2 tablespoons fish sauce
2–4 red chiles, finely sliced, cilantro,
Chinese greens and mint leaves, to
garnish

SERVES 4

1 Pan-fry or broil the sirloin steaks to medium-rare. Set aside to rest for 10–15 minutes.

2 When cool, thinly slice the beef and put the slices in a large bowl.

3 Add the sliced onion, cucumber ribbons and lemongrass.

4 Add the scallions. Toss and season with lime juice and fish sauce. Serve at room temperature or chilled, garnished with the sliced chiles, cilantro, Chinese greens and mint leaves.

THAI-STYLE SWEET-AND-SOUR PORK

Sweet-and-sour is traditionally a Chinese creation, but the Thais also do it very well. This version has an altogether fresher and cleaner flavor, and it makes a good one-dish meal when served over rice.

INGREDIENTS
12 ounces lean pork
2 tablespoons vegetable oil
4 garlic cloves, finely sliced
1 small red onion, sliced
2 tablespoons fish sauce
1 tablespoon sugar
1 red bell pepper, seeded and diced
½ cucumber, seeded and sliced
2 plum tomatoes, cut into wedges
4 ounces pineapple, cut into small chunks
2 scallions, cut into short lengths
freshly ground black pepper
cilantro leaves and scallions, shredded, to garnish

SERVES 4

1 Slice the pork into thin strips. Heat the oil in a wok or large frying pan.

2 Add the garlic and fry until golden, then add the pork and stir-fry for 4–5 minutes. Add the onion.

3 Season with fish sauce, sugar and freshly ground black pepper. Stir and cook for 3–4 minutes or until the pork is cooked.

4 Add the rest of the vegetables, the pineapple and scallions. You may need to add a few tablespoons of water. Continue to stir-fry for another 3–4 minutes. Serve hot, garnished with cilantro leaves and scallions.

RENDANG

his popular Indonesian dish is often served with deep-fried onions and plain boiled rice.

INGREDIENTS
2¼ pounds prime beef in one piece
2 onions or 5–6 shallots, sliced
4 garlic cloves, crushed
1-inch piece fresh lengkuas, peeled and sliced, or 1 teaspoon lengkuas powder
1-inch piece fresh ginger root, peeled and sliced
4–6 fresh red chiles, seeded and sliced
1 lemongrass stalk, lower part, sliced
1-inch piece fresh turmeric, peeled and sliced, or 1 teaspoon ground turmeric
1 teaspoon cilantro seeds, dry-fried and ground
1 teaspoon cumin seeds, dry-fried and ground
2 kaffir lime leaves
1 teaspoon tamarind pulp, soaked in ¼ cup warm water
14-fluid ounce cans coconut milk
1¼ cups water
2 tablespoons dark soy sauce
6–8 small new potatoes, scrubbed
salt
boiled rice and deep-fried onions, to serve

SERVES 6–8

1 Cut the meat in long strips and then into even-size pieces and place in a bowl.

2 Process the onions or shallots, crushed garlic, lengkuas or lengkuas powder, sliced ginger, chopped and deseeded chiles, sliced lemongrass and the fresh or ground turmeric into a fine paste in a food processor. Alternatively, grind finely together using a mortar and pestle.

COOK'S TIP
This dish tastes even better and more flavorful if cooked a day in advance. Follow the recipe up to the end of Step 5; on the next day reheat and add the potatoes and seasoning.

3 Add the paste to the meat with the cilantro and cumin and mix well. Tear the lime leaves and add them to the mixture. Cover and set in a cool place to marinate while you prepare the other ingredients.

4 Strain the tamarind and reserve the juice. Pour the coconut milk, water and tamarind juice into a wok or flameproof casserole and stir in the spiced meat and soy sauce. Add seasoning as desired.

5 Stir until the liquid comes to a boil; then reduce the heat and simmer gently, half-covered, for 1½–2 hours or until the meat is tender and the liquid reduced.

6 Add the potatoes 20–25 minutes before the end of the cooking time. Add a little more water to the pot. Season to taste and serve with rice and deep-fried onions.

STIR-FRIED BEEF WITH ORANGE AND GINGER

Stir-frying uses a minimum of fat, and it's also one of the quickest ways to cook, but you do need to choose very tender meat.

INGREDIENTS
1 pound lean beef rump, fillet or sirloin,
cut into thin strips
finely grated zest and juice of 1 orange
1 tablespoon light soy sauce
1 teaspoon cornstarch
1-inch piece fresh ginger root,
finely chopped
2 teaspoons sesame oil
1 large carrot, cut into thin strips
2 scallions, thinly sliced
rice noodles or boiled rice, to serve

SERVES 4

1 Place the beef strips in a bowl and sprinkle on the orange zest and juice. Cover and let marinate for at least 30 minutes, stirring occasionally.

2 Drain the marinade from the meat and reserve the marinade. Mix the meat with the soy sauce, cornstarch and ginger.

COOK'S TIP
To extract the maximum amount of juice from an orange, warm it for a short while in the oven, then roll it backward and forward with your hand before squeezing.

3 Heat the sesame oil in a wok or large frying pan. When it is hot, add the beef strips and stir-fry for 1 minute, until they are lightly colored. Add the carrot strips and stir-fry for another 2–3 minutes.

4 Stir in the sliced scallions and the reserved marinade, then cook over medium heat, stirring constantly, until the sauce is boiling, thickened and glossy. Serve the stir-fried beef immediately, accompanied by a serving of rice noodles or just plain boiled rice.

DRY-FRIED SHREDDED BEEF

D ry-frying is a unique Szechuan cooking method, in which the main ingredient is first stir-fried slowly over low heat until dry, then finished off quickly with the other ingredients over high heat.

INGREDIENTS
12–14 ounces lean beef
1 large or 2 small carrots
2–3 celery stalks
2 tablespoons sesame oil
1 tablespoon Chinese rice wine or
dry sherry
1 tablespoon hot bean sauce
1 tablespoon light soy sauce
1 garlic clove, finely chopped
1 teaspoon light brown sugar
2–3 scallions, finely chopped
½ teaspoon finely chopped fresh
ginger root
ground Szechuan peppercorns, to taste

SERVES 4

1 Using a cleaver or a very sharp knife, slice the beef into matchstick shreds. Thinly shred the carrots and celery into pieces about the same size.

2 Heat a wok, then add the sesame oil (it will smoke very quickly). Reduce the heat and stir-fry the beef shreds with the wine or sherry until the color changes.

3 Pour off the excess liquid from the wok and reserve. Continue stirring until the meat is absolutely dry.

4 Add the hot bean sauce, soy sauce, garlic and sugar. Blend thoroughly, then add the carrot and celery shreds.

5 Increase the heat to high and add the scallions, ginger and the reserved cooking liquid. Continue stirring and, when all the juice has evaporated, season with Szechuan pepper and serve.

STIR-FRIED PORK WITH VEGETABLES

This is a basic recipe for cooking any meat with any vegetables in an authentic Chinese style. It can be varied according to seasonal availability.

INGREDIENTS

8 ounces pork tenderloin

1 tablespoon light soy sauce

1 teaspoon light brown sugar

1 teaspoon Chinese rice wine or dry sherry

2 teaspoons cornstarch mixed with a little water

4 ounces snowpeas

4 ounces mushrooms

1 large or 2 small carrots

1 scallion

1/4 cup vegetable oil

1 teaspoon salt

chicken stock or water, if necessary

few drops of sesame oil, to serve

SERVES 4

1 Cut the pork into thin 1-inch slices. Marinate with about 1 teaspoon of the soy sauce, the sugar, wine or sherry and cornstarch paste.

2 Trim the snowpeas; thinly slice the mushrooms; cut the carrots into pieces roughly the same size as the pork, and cut the scallions diagonally into short sections.

3 Heat a wok, then add the oil. When it is hot, add the pork and stir-fry for about 1 minute or until its color changes. Remove with a slotted spoon and keep warm.

4 Put the prepared vegetables into the wok and cook, stirring and turning, for about 2 minutes.

5 Add the salt and the partly cooked pork, and a little stock or water only if necessary. Continue stirring for another 1–2 minutes, then add the remaining soy sauce and blend thoroughly. Sprinkle with sesame oil and serve immediately.

Mu Shu Pork with Eggs and Mushrooms

I n Chinese *Mu Shu* is the name for a bright yellow flower. Traditionally, this dish is served as a filling wrapped in thin pancakes, but it can also be served on its own with plain rice.

INGREDIENTS

½ ounce dried wood-ear mushrooms
6–8 ounces pork tenderloin
8 ounces Chinese cabbage
4 ounces canned bamboo shoots, drained
2 scallions
3 eggs
1 teaspoon salt
¼ cup vegetable oil
1 tablespoon light soy sauce
1 tablespoon Chinese rice wine or dry sherry
few drops of sesame oil, to serve

SERVES 4

1 Soak the mushrooms in a bowl of cold water for 25–30 minutes, then rinse thoroughly and discard any hard stems. Drain the mushrooms, then thinly slice. Cut the pork into matchstick pieces. Thinly shred the Chinese cabbage, bamboo shoots and scallions.

2 Break the eggs into a bowl, add a pinch of salt, and beat. Heat a little oil in a wok, add the eggs and stir and turn gently until lightly scrambled but not at all dry. Remove, set aside and keep warm.

3 Heat the remaining oil in the wok, add the pork and stir-fry for about 1 minute or until the color changes. Add the mushrooms, Chinese cabbage, bamboo shoots and scallions and stir-fry for another minute, then add the remaining salt, the soy sauce, and wine or sherry.

4 Stir-fry the vegetables for another minute before returning the scrambled eggs to the wok. Break up the eggs and blend in well. Sprinkle with sesame oil and serve immediately.

GINGER PORK WITH BLACK BEAN SAUCE

T he combination of the sweetness of peppers and the saltiness of preserved black beans gives this Chinese dish a wonderful, distinctive flavor.

INGREDIENTS
12 ounces pork fillet
1 garlic clove, crushed
1 tablespoon grated fresh ginger root
6 tablespoons chicken stock
2 tablespoons dry sherry
1 tablespoon light soy sauce
1 teaspoon sugar
2 teaspoons cornstarch
3 tablespoons peanut oil
2 yellow bell peppers, seeded and cut into strips
2 red bell peppers, seeded and cut into strips
1 bunch scallions, sliced diagonally
3 tablespoons preserved black beans, coarsely chopped
cilantro, to garnish (optional)

SERVES 4

1 Cut the pork into thin slices across the grain of the meat. Put the slices into a bowl and mix them with the garlic and ginger. Let marinate at room temperature for 15 minutes.

2 Blend together the stock, sherry, soy sauce, sugar and cornstarch in a small bowl, then set the sauce mixture aside.

3 Heat the oil in a wok or large frying pan, add the marinated pork and stir-fry for 2–3 minutes. Add the peppers and scallions and stir-fry for another 2 minutes *(left)*. Add the beans and sauce mixture and cook, stirring, until thick. Serve hot, garnished with cilantro, if using.

STEAK BOWL

This Japanese dish looks very good at a dinner party, and it is also very easy to prepare, leaving the cook with time to relax.

INGREDIENTS
1 large mild onion
1 red bell pepper, seeded
2 tablespoons oil
2 tablespoons butter
14 ounces sirloin steak, trimmed of excess fat
¼ cup ketchup
2 tablespoons Worcestershire sauce
2 tablespoons chopped parsley
7 cups freshly boiled Japanese rice
salt and freshly ground black pepper
bunch of watercress, to garnish

SERVES 4

1 Cut the onion and red pepper into ⅓-inch slices.

2 Heat 1 tablespoon of the oil in a frying pan and cook the onion slices until golden on both sides, adding salt and pepper, then set aside.

3 Heat the remaining oil and 1 tablespoon of the butter. Cook the steak over high heat until browned on both sides, then cut it into bite-size pieces and set aside. For well-done steak, cook it over medium heat for 1–2 minutes on each side.

4 Mix the ketchup, Worcestershire sauce and 2 tablespoons water in the pan in which the steak was cooked. Stir over medium heat for 1 minute, mixing in the meat residue.

5 Mix the remaining butter and the chopped parsley into the hot rice. Divide among four serving bowls. Top the rice with the red pepper, onion and steak, and pour on the sauce. Garnish with watercress.

BEEF AND VEGETABLES ON A HOT PLATE

This is *Yakiniku*, a dish of beef cooked at the table—you will need a portable griddle or frying pan and you can cook a variety of different ingredients, such as chicken or fish.

INGREDIENTS

1 oak leaf lettuce
1 daikon, finely grated
oil, for cooking
14-ounce beef topside, very thinly sliced
1 red bell pepper, seeded and sliced
1 green bell pepper, seeded and sliced
1 large mild onion, sliced into rings
4 shiitake mushrooms, stems removed
1 carrot, thinly sliced
*8 raw jumbo shrimp, heads removed,
shelled, with tails left on*
soy sauce, to serve

FOR THE PONZU DIP
*generous ⅓ cup each of lemon juice, soy
sauce and instant dashi*

SERVES 4

1 Prepare the dip by mixing all the ingredients. Divide the dip among four small individual serving bowls. Separate the lettuce leaves and arrange them on plates.

2 Gently squeeze the grated daikon to remove any excess water. Place 1–2 tablespoons daikon into four small individual serving bowls and pour on a little soy sauce.

3 Heat the broiler or a hot plate on a thick mat to protect the table. Add a little oil and quickly cook the beef until it is cooked on both sides. Grill the peppers, onion, shiitake mushrooms, carrot and shrimp at the same time.

4 To eat the food, wrap individual portions in lettuce leaves and dip them into the ponzu or daikon dip. Alternatively, the food may be dipped without being wrapped in the lettuce leaves, if desired.

COOK'S TIP
This recipe is an example of a party meal, an essential part of Japanese home entertainment. Dishes are cooked at the table so guests can participate in cooking their own food.

VEGETABLE-STUFFED BEEF ROLLS

Thinly sliced meats are used almost daily in Japanese cooking, so there are countless recipes for them. These stuffed beef rolls, or *Yahata-maki*, are very popular for picnic meals. You can roll up other vegetables in the beef, such as asparagus tips, and you can also replace the beef with pork.

INGREDIENTS
2 ounces carrot
2 ounces green bell pepper, seeded
bunch of scallions
14-ounce beef topside, thinly sliced
all-purpose flour, for dusting
1 tablespoon oil
fresh parsley sprigs, to garnish

FOR THE SAUCE
2 tablespoons sugar
3 tablespoons soy sauce
3 tablespoons mirin

SERVES 4

1 Shred the carrot and green pepper into 1½–2-inch lengths. Halve the scallions lengthwise, then shred them diagonally into similar-size lengths.

2 The beef slices should be 1/12 inch thick, no thicker, and about 6 inches square. Lay a slice of beef on a cutting board and top it with carrot, green pepper and scallion strips. Roll it up quite tightly and dust it lightly with flour. Repeat the process with the remaining beef and sliced vegetables.

3 Heat the oil in a frying pan. Add the beef rolls, placing the seams underneath to prevent them from unrolling. Fry them over medium heat until golden and cooked, turning occasionally.

4 Add the sauce ingredients to the frying pan and increase the heat. Roll the beef quickly to glaze the rolls.

5 Remove the rolls from the pan and halve them, cutting at a slant. Stand the rolls, with the sloping cut end facing upward on a plate. Dress with the sauce and garnish with parsley. Serve hot or cold.

DEEP-FRIED PORK STRIPS WITH SHREDDED CABBAGE

Deep-fried pork is very tasty when served with soft green cabbage and a fruity sauce, known as *tonkatsu*. This dish is enjoyed throughout Japan.

INGREDIENTS
4 boneless pork loin steaks, 4 ounces each
1¹/₂ teaspoons salt
freshly ground black pepper
all-purpose flour, for coating
2 eggs, very lightly beaten
2 ounces fresh white bread crumbs
¹/₂ soft green cabbage, finely shredded
oil, for deep frying

FOR THE TONKATSU SAUCE
generous ¹/₃ cup brown sauce (select
a fruity brand)
3 tablespoons ketchup
1 tablespoon sugar

SERVES 4

COOK'S TIP
Commercial Japanese *tonkatsu* sauce is available ready-prepared, and it may be substituted for the sauce ingredients listed above.

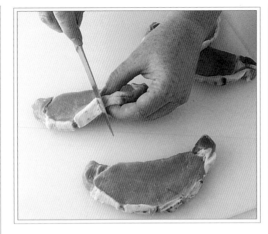

1 Snip any fat off the pork steaks to ensure that the meat remains flat when frying. Then, beat the pork with a meat mallet or a rolling pin to tenderize it. Season with the salt and black pepper, and dust the pork lightly with flour.

2 Dip the steaks into the lightly beaten egg first, and then coat them all over with the bread crumbs. Press the bread crumbs onto the steaks with your fingers to ensure that they stick well. Refrigerate them for about 10 minutes, as chilling will give the coating time to set slightly.

3 Meanwhile, soak the shredded green cabbage in a bowl of cold water for about 5 minutes. Make sure that it is well drained, and chill until needed.

4 Combine the ingredients for the *tonkatsu* sauce in a bowl. Stir constantly, and make sure that all the sugar has properly dissolved.

5 Slowly heat the oil for deep-frying to 330–340°F. Deep-fry two steaks at a time for about 6 minutes, turning them until they are crisp and golden.

6 Skim any floating bread crumbs from the oil occasionally to prevent them from burning. Drain the steaks well on dish towels and keep hot.

7 Cut the steaks into ³/₄-inch strips and place them on a plate. Arrange the chilled cabbage beside the pork and pour on the sauce . Serve immediately.

VEGETABLE DISHES

People who eat in Asian restaurants know about the wide variety of vegetable dishes available, making these favorite places for vegetarians to dine. Okra, spinach, potatoes, mushrooms, cauliflower and eggplants all feature highly in Indian and Balti dishes and these authentic recipes are easy to prepare.

Tofu is another widely used ingredient in Asian cookery. Made from the pressed curd of the soya bean, tofu is low in fat and rich in protein, making it perfect for vegetarians. It can be prepared in dozens of ways: boiled, stir-fried or deep-fried are just three methods described in this chapter for you to try.

SPICED OKRA WITH ALMONDS

Long and elegantly shaped, it's not surprising that these vegetables are commonly called "lady's fingers." Native to tropical Africa, they are very popular in India and Arab countries.

INGREDIENTS
½ cup blanched almonds, chopped
2 tablespoons butter
8 ounces okra
1 tablespoon sunflower oil
2 garlic cloves, crushed
1-inch piece fresh ginger root, grated
1 teaspoon cumin seeds
1 teaspoon ground cilantro
1 teaspoon paprika
1¼ cups water
salt and ground black pepper

SERVES 2–4

1 In a shallow flameproof dish, fry the almonds in the butter until they are lightly golden. Remove from the pan with a slotted spoon and drain on paper towels.

2 Using a sharp knife, trim the tops of the okra stems and around the edges of the stalks. The pods contain a sticky liquid that oozes out if they are prepared too far in advance, so trim them just before cooking. Heat the oil in the pan, add the okra and stir-fry, with a wooden spoon, for 2 minutes, until the okra starts to soften.

3 Add the garlic and ginger, and fry gently for 1 minute, then add the cumin seeds, cilantro and paprika and cook for another 1–2 minutes, stirring constantly.

4 Pour in the measured water. Season generously with salt and pepper, cover the pan and simmer for about 5 minutes, until the okra feels just tender when pierced with the tip of a sharp knife. Stir the mixture occasionally.

5 Finally, stir in the fried almonds and serve the dish piping hot.

SPICED EGGPLANT

The exact origins of the eggplant are uncertain, but it has been cultivated in India since ancient times. It comes from the same family as the potato and is related to both the petunia and the tobacco plant.

INGREDIENTS
2 eggplant, halved lengthwise
salt
¼ cup olive oil, plus extra if needed
2 large onions, thinly sliced
2 garlic cloves, crushed
1 green bell pepper, seeded and sliced
14-ounce can chopped tomatoes
3 tablespoons sugar
1 teaspoon ground cilantro
ground black pepper
2 tablespoons chopped cilantro
or parsley
cilantro sprigs, to garnish
crusty bread, to serve

SERVES 4

1 Using a sharp knife, slash the flesh of the eggplant a few times. Sprinkle with salt and drain in a colander for about 30 minutes. Rinse well and pat dry.

2 Gently cook the eggplant, cut-side down, in the oil for 5 minutes, then drain and place in a shallow ovenproof dish.

3 In the same pan, gently sauté the onions, garlic and green pepper, adding extra oil if necessary. Cook for about 10 minutes, stirring occasionally, until all the vegetables have softened.

4 Add the tomatoes, sugar, ground cilantro and black pepper to the onion and green pepper mixture. Stir to combine thoroughly, then cook for about 5 minutes, until the mixture is reduced. Stir in the chopped cilantro or parsley.

5 Preheat the oven to 375°F. Spoon the mixture on top of the halved eggplant, cover and bake for 30–35 minutes. Cool, garnish with cilantro sprigs, and serve cold with crusty bread.

COOK'S TIP
Sprinkling the cut surfaces of eggplant with salt lets the juices that form drain away in a colander. Before cooking, it is important to rinse the eggplant well and pat dry with paper towels. Prepared like this, eggplant is less bitter.

SPICED SPINACH AND POTATOES

I ndia has more than 18 varieties of spinach. If you have access to an Indian or Chinese supermarket, it is well worth looking for some of the more unusual varieties.

INGREDIENTS

1 pound potatoes

¼ cup vegetable oil

1-inch piece fresh ginger root, grated

4 garlic cloves, crushed

1 onion, coarsely chopped

2 green chiles, chopped

2 whole dried red chiles,
coarsely broken

1 teaspoon cumin seeds

8 ounces fresh spinach, chopped
or 8 ounces frozen spinach,
thawed and drained

salt

2 firm tomatoes, peeled and coarsely
chopped, to garnish

SERVES 4–6

1 Cut large potatoes into quarters or, if using small new potatoes, leave them whole. Heat the oil in a frying pan and cook the potatoes until brown on all sides. Remove from the pan and set aside.

2 Pour off the excess oil from the pan, leaving 1 tablespoon. Add the ginger, garlic, onion, green and red chiles and cumin seeds and sauté gently until the onion is golden brown.

3 Add the potatoes, season with salt, and stir well. Cook, covered, until the potatoes are tender when pierced with the point of a sharp knife.

4 Add the spinach and stir well to mix with the potatoes. Cook, uncovered, until the spinach is tender and all the excess liquid has evaporated. Garnish with the chopped tomatoes and serve hot.

SPICY CABBAGE

An excellent side dish, this cabbage dish is very versatile and can even be served as a warm side salad or cold with a selection of cold meats. Try red cabbage for a change.

INGREDIENTS
¼ cup margarine or butter
½ teaspoon white cumin seeds
3–8 dried red chiles, to taste
1 small onion, sliced
2½ cups shredded cabbage
2 carrots, grated
½ teaspoon salt
2 tablespoons lemon juice

SERVES 4

1 Put the margarine or butter into a saucepan and heat until melted. Add the cumin seeds. Crumble in the dried chiles and fry, stirring, for about 30 seconds.

2 Add the onion to the pan and sauté for about 2 minutes. Add the cabbage and carrots and stir-fry for another 5 minutes or until the cabbage is soft.

3 Finally, stir in the salt and lemon juice. Taste for seasoning, then transfer to a warmed serving dish and serve immediately.

KARAHI SHREDDED CABBAGE WITH CUMIN

This cabbage dish is only lightly spiced and makes a good accompaniment to most other Indian and western dishes.

INGREDIENTS

1 tablespoon corn oil
¼ cup butter
½ teaspoon crushed cilantro seeds
½ teaspoon white cumin seeds
6 dried red chiles
1 small Savoy cabbage, shredded
12 snowpeas
12 ears baby corn
3 fresh red chiles, seeded and sliced
salt, to taste
¼ cup sliced almonds, toasted and
1 tablespoon chopped fresh
cilantro, to garnish

SERVES 4

1 Heat the oil with the butter in a deep, round frying pan or a karahi. When it is hot, add the crushed cilantro seeds, white cumin seeds and dried red chiles and stir-fry for 1 minute.

2 Add the shredded cabbage and snowpeas and stir-fry for about 5 minutes.

3 Add the baby corn, chiles *(right),* and salt and cook for 3 minutes, until the vegetables are tender.

4 Garnish with the toasted almonds and cilantro, and serve hot.

CAULIFLOWER WITH COCONUT

I n this dish, the creamy coconut sauce is the perfect contrast to the spiced cauliflower. Serve as a side-dish to traditional Indian dishes.

INGREDIENTS

1 tablespoon all-purpose flour
½ cup water
1 teaspoon chili powder
1 tablespoon ground cilantro
1 teaspoon ground cumin
1 teaspoon mustard powder
1 teaspoon ground turmeric
¼ cup vegetable oil
6–8 curry leaves
1 teaspoon cumin seeds
1 cauliflower, broken into florets
¾ cup thick coconut milk
juice of 2 lemons
salt
lime wedges, to garnish

SERVES 4–6

1 Mix the flour with a little of the water to make a smooth paste. Add the chili powder, cilantro, cumin, mustard, turmeric and salt to taste. Add the remaining water and keep mixing to blend all the ingredients well.

2 Heat the oil in a frying pan and fry the curry leaves and cumin seeds. Add the spice paste and simmer for about 5 minutes. If the sauce has become too thick, add a little hot water.

3 Add the cauliflower and coconut milk. Bring to a boil, cover and simmer until the cauliflower is tender but crunchy. Add the lemon juice, mix well, and serve hot garnished with lime wedges.

MIXED VEGETABLES IN COCONUT MILK

A most delicious way of cooking vegetables. If you don't like highly spiced food, use fewer red chiles.

INGREDIENTS
1 pound mixed vegetables, such as
eggplant, baby corn, carrots, snake beans
and patty pan squash
8 red chiles, seeded
2 lemongrass stalks, chopped
4 kaffir lime leaves, torn
2 tablespoons vegetable oil
1 cup coconut milk
2 tablespoons fish sauce
salt
15–20 Thai basil leaves, to garnish

SERVES 4–6

1 Cut the vegetables into similar-size shapes using a sharp knife.

2 Put the red chiles, lemongrass and kaffir lime leaves in a mortar and grind together with a pestle.

3 Heat the oil in a wok or large, deep, frying pan. Add the chili mixture and fry for 2–3 minutes.

4 Stir in the coconut milk and bring to a boil. Add the vegetables and cook for about 5 minutes or until they are tender. Season with the fish sauce and salt, and garnish with Thai basil leaves.

BAMBOO SHOOT SALAD

T his salad, which has a hot and sharp flavor, originated in Northeast Thailand. Use fresh, young bamboo shoots when you can find them, otherwise substitute canned bamboo shoots.

INGREDIENTS
14-ounce can whole bamboo shoots
1 ounce glutinous rice
2 tablespoons chopped shallots
1 tablespoon chopped garlic
3 tablespoons chopped scallions
2 tablespoons fish sauce
2 tablespoons lime juice
1 teaspoon sugar
½ teaspoon dried flaked chiles
20–25 small mint leaves
1 tablespoon toasted sesame seeds

SERVES 4

1 Rinse and drain the bamboo shoots, finely slice and set aside.

2 Dry-roast the rice in a frying pan until it is golden brown. Remove and grind to fine crumbs with a mortar and pestle.

3 Put the rice in a bowl, add the shallots, garlic, scallions, fish sauce, lime juice, sugar, chiles and half the mint leaves.

4 Mix thoroughly, then pour over the bamboo shoots and toss together. Serve sprinkled with sesame seeds and the remaining mint leaves.

TOFU AND GREEN BEAN RED CURRY

This is another curry that is simple and quick to make. This recipe uses green beans, but you can use almost any kind of vegetable, such as eggplant, bamboo shoots or broccoli.

INGREDIENTS

2½ cups coconut milk
1 tablespoon red curry paste
3 tablespoons fish sauce
2 teaspoons palm sugar
8 ounces button mushrooms
4 ounces green beans, trimmed
6 ounces tofu, rinsed and
cut into ¾-inch cubes
4 kaffir lime leaves, torn
2 red chiles, sliced
cilantro leaves, to garnish

SERVES 4–6

1 Put about one-third of the coconut milk in a wok or saucepan. Cook until it starts to separate and an oily sheen appears.

2 Add the red curry paste, fish sauce and sugar to the coconut milk. Combine.

3 Add the mushrooms to the curry sauce. Stir and cook for 1 minute.

4 Stir in the rest of the coconut milk and bring back to a boil.

5 Add the green beans and tofu and simmer gently for another 4–5 minutes.

6 Stir in the torn kaffir lime leaves and sliced chiles. Serve garnished with the cilantro leaves.

TOFU STIR-FRY

Tofu has a pleasant creamy texture, which makes a good contrast with crunchy stir-fried vegetables. It is favored by vegetarians, as it is an excellent meat substitute, high in protein and low in fat. Make sure you buy firm tofu, which cuts easily.

INGREDIENTS

4 ounces hard white cabbage
2 green chiles
8 ounces firm tofu
3 tablespoons vegetable oil
2 cloves garlic, crushed
3 scallions, chopped
6 ounces green beans, trimmed
6 ounces baby corn, halved
4 ounces bean sprouts
3 tablespoons smooth peanut butter
1½ tablespoons dark soy sauce
1¼ cups coconut milk

SERVES 2–4

1 Shred the white cabbage thinly and set aside. Carefully remove the seeds from the chiles, chop the flesh finely and set aside. Cut the tofu into thin strips about ½ inches thick.

2 Heat the wok, then add 2 tablespoons of the oil. When the oil is hot, add the tofu, stir-fry for 3 minutes and remove. Set aside. Wipe out the wok with paper towels.

3 Add the remaining oil. When it is hot, add the garlic, cabbage, scallions and chiles and stir-fry for 1 minute. Add the green beans, corn and bean-sprouts and stir-fry for another 2 minutes.

4 Add the peanut butter and soy sauce. Stir well to coat the vegetables. Add the tofu to the vegetables.

5 Pour the coconut milk over the vegetables, simmer for 3 minutes and serve immediately.

CABBAGE SALAD

A simple and delicious way of using cabbage. Other vegetables such as broccoli, cauliflower and Chinese cabbage can also be used.

INGREDIENTS
2 tablespoons fish sauce
grated zest of 1 lime
2 tablespoons lime juice
$\frac{1}{2}$ cup coconut milk
2 tablespoons vegetable oil
2 large red chiles, seeded and
cut into fine strips
6 garlic cloves, finely sliced
6 shallots, finely sliced
1 small cabbage, shredded
2 tablespoons coarsely chopped
roasted peanuts, to serve

SERVES 4–6

1 Make the dressing by combining the fish sauce, lime zest and juice and coconut milk. Set aside.

2 Heat the oil in a wok or frying pan. Stir-fry the chiles, garlic and shallots, until the shallots are brown and crisp. Remove and set aside.

3 Blanch the cabbage in boiling salted water for 2–3 minutes, drain and put into a bowl.

4 Stir the dressing into the cabbage, toss and mix well. Transfer the salad into a serving dish. Sprinkle with the fried shallot mixture and the chopped roasted peanuts.

STIR-FRIED MIXED VEGETABLES

When selecting different items for a dish, never mix ingredients indiscriminately. In their cooking, as in all things, the Chinese aim to achieve a harmonious balance of color and texture.

INGREDIENTS
8 ounces Chinese cabbage
4 ounces baby corn
4 ounces broccoli
1 large or 2 small carrots
¼ cup vegetable oil
1 teaspoon salt
1 teaspoon light brown sugar
chicken stock or water, if necessary
1 tablespoon light soy sauce
few drops of sesame oil (optional)

SERVES 4

1 Cut the Chinese cabbage into thick slices. Cut the ears of corn lengthwise, if desired. Separate the broccoli into florets and slice the carrots diagonally.

2 Heat the oil in a wok, add the Chinese cabbage, corn, broccoli and carrots and stir-fry for about 2 minutes.

3 Add the salt and sugar, and a little stock or water, if necessary, so the vegetables do not dry out, and continue stirring for another minute (*left*). Add the soy sauce and sesame oil, if using. Blend well into the vegetable mixture and serve immediately.

FRUIT AND RAW VEGETABLE GADO-GADO

his tangy, fresh salad is ideal before a spicy main course, or to accompany a creamy curry.

INGREDIENTS
2 unripe pears, peeled at the last minute
1–2 apples
juice of ½ lemon
1 small, crisp lettuce or a banana leaf
½ cucumber, seeded, sliced and salted, set aside for 15 minutes, then rinsed and drained
6 small tomatoes, cut into wedges
3 slices fresh pineapple, cored and cut into wedges
3 eggs or 12 quail's eggs, hard-boiled and shelled
6 ounces egg noodles, cooked, cooled and chopped
deep-fried onions, to garnish

FOR THE PEANUT SAUCE
1 tablespoon tamarind pulp
2–4 fresh red chiles, seeded and ground
1¼ cups coconut milk
12 ounces crunchy peanut butter
1 tablespoon dark soy sauce
salt
coarsely crushed peanuts, to garnish

SERVES 6

1 To make the peanut sauce, soak the tamarind pulp in 3 tablespoons warm water, strain and reserve the juice. Put the chiles and coconut milk in a saucepan. Add the peanut butter and heat gently, stirring, until smooth.

2 Let simmer gently until the sauce thickens, then add the soy sauce and the tamarind juice. Season with salt to taste. Pour into a bowl and garnish with a few coarsely crushed peanuts.

3 To make the salad, peel and core the pears and apples, slice them and sprinkle the apples with lemon juice. Shred the lettuce leaves to form a bed for the salad in a shallow bowl or flat platter. Alternatively line with the whole banana leaf. Arrange the fruit and vegetables attractively on top.

4 Add the sliced or quartered hard-boiled eggs (leave quail's eggs whole) and the chopped noodles. Garnish with the deep-fried onions.

5 Serve immediately, accompanied with a bowl of the peanut sauce.

COOK'S TIP
Any fruit or vegetable can be substituted for the ones mentioned here. Experiment with soft, sweet tropical fruits such as mango or lychees, combined with sharp fruits such as grapefruit or lemon, for extra zing, and an authentic sweet and sour experience.

BOK CHOY AND MUSHROOM STIR-FRY

T ry to buy all the types of mushrooms, if you can, as the variety of flavors gives great subtlety to the finished dish; the oyster and shiitake mushrooms have particularly distinctive flavors.

INGREDIENTS

4 dried black Chinese mushrooms
1 pound bok choy
2 ounces oyster mushrooms
2 ounces shiitake mushrooms
1 tablespoon vegetable oil
1 garlic clove, crushed
2 tablespoons oyster sauce

SERVES 4

COOK'S TIP

Bok choy is a type of cabbage with long thin stems and dark green leaves. The leaves are crisp and the flavor is very distinctive.

1 Put the dried black Chinese mushrooms into a small bowl and pour in ⅔ cup boiling water. Set aside for about 15 minutes to let them soften.

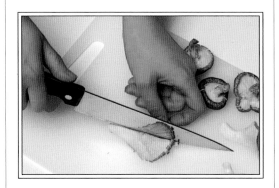

2 Meanwhile, tear the bok choy into bite-size pieces with your fingers. Using a sharp knife, halve any large oyster or shiitake mushrooms, using a sharp knife.

3 Strain the Chinese mushrooms. Heat the wok, then add the oil. When hot, stir-fry the garlic until softened but not colored.

4 Add the bok choy and stir-fry for about 1 minute. Mix in all the mushrooms and stir-fry for 1 minute. Finally, add the oyster sauce, toss well and serve immediately.

VARIATION

Braise the mushrooms in a well-flavored sauce. Omit the bok choy. Heat 1 tablespoon oil in a wok, add a selection of mushrooms and stir-fry for 1 minute, then add 2 tablespoons each of dark soy sauce, Chinese rice wine or dry sherry and sugar, 1 teaspoon sesame oil and 1¼ cups chicken or vegetable stock. Reduce the heat and braise, stirring for 5–7 minutes, until the liquid has almost evaporated.

STIR-FRIED BRUSSELS SPROUTS

An interesting way to cook Brussels sprouts, this method works equally well with shredded green cabbage. It is a recipe which also goes very well with European meals.

INGREDIENTS
1 pound Brussels sprouts, shredded
1 teaspoon sesame or sunflower oil
2 scallions, sliced
½ teaspoon five-spice powder
1 tablespoon light soy sauce
sliced scallions, to garnish

SERVES 4

1 Trim the Brussels sprouts and remove any loose or yellowing leaves, then shred them finely, either using a large sharp knife or in a food processor.

2 Heat a wok or frying pan and then add the oil. When it is hot, add the Brussels sprouts and scallions, and stir-fry for about 2 minutes, without letting the vegetables brown.

3 Stir in the five-spice powder and soy sauce (*left*), then cook, stirring, for another 2–3 minutes, until just tender. Serve immediately, garnished with the sliced scallions.

168

CRISPY SEAWEED

I n northern China they use a special kind of seaweed for this dish, but spring greens, shredded very finely, make a very good alternative. Serve either as an appetizer or as a side dish.

INGREDIENTS
8 ounces spring greens
peanut or corn oil, for deep-frying
¼ teaspoon salt
2 teaspoons light brown sugar
2–3 tablespoons sliced toasted almonds,
to garnish

SERVES 4

1 Cut out and discard any tough stalks from the spring greens. Place about six leaves on top of each other and roll up tightly. Using a sharp knife, slice across into very thin shreds. Lay on a tray and let dry for about 2 hours.

2 Heat 2–3 inches of oil in a heavy saucepan or wok to 375°F. Carefully place a handful of the leaves in the oil—it will bubble and spit for about the first 10 seconds and then die down. Deep-fry the leaves for about 45 seconds or until they are a slightly darker green—do not let the leaves burn.

3 Remove the leaves with a slotted spoon, drain on paper towels and transfer to a serving dish. Keep warm in the oven while frying the remainder.

4 When you have deep-fried all the shredded leaves, sprinkle them with the salt and sugar and toss lightly so that they are all thoroughly coated. Garnish with the toasted almonds and serve immediately.

COOK'S TIP
Make sure that your pan is deep enough to let the oil bubble up during cooking. The pan should be less than half full.

TOFU AND CRUNCHY VEGETABLES

Tofu is best if it is marinated lightly before cooking to add extra flavor. Using smoked tofu makes this Chinese dish even tastier.

INGREDIENTS
8-ounces carton smoked tofu, cubed
3 tablespoons soy sauce
2 tablespoons dry sherry or vermouth
1 tablespoon sesame oil
3 tablespoons peanut
or sunflower oil
2 leeks, thinly sliced
2 carrots, cut into sticks
1 large zucchini, thinly sliced
4 ounces baby corn, halved
4 ounces button or shiitake
mushrooms, sliced
1 tablespoon sesame seeds
egg noodles, to serve

SERVES 4

COOK'S TIP
The secret of successful stir-frying is to have all your ingredients ready prepared before you heat the oil in the wok. Arrange vegetables on separate dishes and measure out sauces, oils and spices.

1 Place the tofu cubes in a large bowl and add the soy sauce, sherry or vermouth and the sesame oil. Stir to mix thoroughly, then cover and let marinate in a cool place for at least 30 minutes. Lift the tofu cubes out of the marinade with a slotted spoon, reserving the marinade.

2 Heat the peanut or sunflower oil in a wok or large frying pan, add the tofu cubes and stir-fry until browned all over. Remove with a slotted spoon and set aside.

3 Stir-fry the leeks, carrots, zucchini and baby corn, stirring and tossing for about 2 minutes. Add the mushrooms and stir-fry for another minute.

4 Return the tofu cubes to the wok and pour in the reserved marinade. Heat until bubbling, then sprinkle on the sesame seeds. Serve immediately, straight from the wok, with hot noodles tossed in a little sesame oil if desired.

BRAISED VEGETABLES

The original recipe calls for no fewer than 18 different ingredients to represent the 18 Buddhas. Later, this was reduced to eight, but nowadays anything between four and six items is regarded as more than sufficient.

INGREDIENTS

¼ ounce dried wood-ear mushrooms
3 ounces straw mushrooms, drained
3 ounces sliced bamboo shoots, drained
2 ounces snowpeas
8 ounces tofu
6 ounces Chinese cabbage
3–4 tablespoons vegetable oil
1 teaspoon salt
½ teaspoon light brown sugar
1 tablespoon light soy sauce
few drops of sesame oil (optional)

SERVES 4

1 Soak the wood-ear mushrooms in cold water for 20–25 minutes, then rinse and discard the hard stems, if any. Cut the straw mushrooms in half lengthwise; if large cut in pieces, if small keep them whole. Rinse and drain the bamboo shoot slices. Trim the snowpeas. Cut the tofu into about 12 small pieces. Cut the cabbage into pieces about the same size as the snowpeas.

2 Harden the tofu pieces by placing them in a saucepan of boiling water for about 2 minutes. Remove and drain.

3 Heat the oil in a wok or frying pan. When it is hot, add the tofu pieces and lightly brown on all sides. Remove with a slotted spoon and keep warm.

4 Add the wood-ear and straw mushrooms, bamboo shoots, snowpeas and Chinese cabbage to the wok or frying pan and stir-fry for about 1½ minutes, then add the tofu pieces, salt, sugar and soy sauce. Continue stirring for another minute, then cover and braise for 2–3 minutes. Sprinkle with sesame oil, if using, transfer to a warmed platter and serve.

COOK'S TIP
When using dried mushrooms, first rinse them under cold running water to remove any grit, then soak in a bowl with water to cover by 2 inches.

GREEN BEANS WITH SESAME SEEDS

This excellent Japanese dish is flavored with a delicious Gomaae sauce made predominantly from sesame seeds. Serve it with other vegetables, such as spinach, if desired.

INGREDIENTS
7 ounces green beans
salt

FOR THE GOMAAE SAUCE
¹/₄ cup white sesame seeds
2 teaspoons sugar
1 tablespoon soy sauce
1 tablespoon instant dashi

SERVES 4

1 Trim the beans and then cook them in boiling salted water for about 2 minutes or until they are tender.

2 Drain the cooked beans and soak them in cold water for 1 minute to preserve their color. Drain well and cut into lengths of 1¹/₄–1¹/₂ inches. Chill for 5 minutes.

3 To make the sauce, grind the white sesame seeds in a mortar and pestle, leaving some of the sesame seeds whole. Alternatively, roughly chop the sesame seeds on a cutting board with a knife.

4 Put the ground white sesame seeds into a small mixing bowl and carefully stir in the sugar. Then add the soy sauce and the instant dashi. Combine all the ingredients well with a rubber spatula.

5 To serve, put the chilled beans in a large mixing bowl, add the sauce and toss well. Transfer the beans to four small bowls, and serve immediately.

MIXED VEGETABLE SOUP

he main ingredient for this soup is crushed tofu, which is both nutritious and filling.

INGREDIENTS
5 ounces fresh Japanese tofu
2 dried shiitake mushrooms
2 ounces burdock
1 teaspoon rice vinegar
½ black or white konnyaku, 4¼ ounces
2 tablespoons sesame oil
4 ounces daikon, thinly sliced
2 ounces carrot, thinly sliced
scant 3 cups kombu and bonito stock
or instant dashi
pinch of salt
2 tablespoons sake or dry white wine
1½ teaspoons mirin
3 tablespoons white or red miso paste
dash of soy sauce
6 snowpeas, trimmed, boiled and thinly sliced, to garnish

SERVES 4

1 Crush the tofu by hand until it resembles a lumpy scrambled egg texture—do not crush it too finely.

2 Wrap the tofu in a dish cloth and put it in a strainer, then pour in plenty of boiling water. Let the tofu drain thoroughly for 10 minutes.

3 Soak the dried shiitake mushrooms in tepid water for 20 minutes, then drain them, reserving the soaking water for stock. Remove their stems, and cut the caps into four to six pieces.

4 Use a vegetable brush to scrub the skin off the burdock and slice it carefully into thin shavings. Soak the shavings for about 5 minutes in plenty of cold water with the vinegar added to remove any bitter taste. Drain well.

5 Put the konnyaku in a small saucepan and pour in just enough water to cover it. Bring to a boil over medium heat, then drain and let cool. Using your hands, tear the konnyaku into ¾-inch lumps. Do not use a knife, as smooth cuts will prevent it from absorbing flavor.

6 Heat the sesame oil in a deep saucepan. Add all the shiitake mushrooms, gobo, daikon, carrot and konnyaku. Stir-fry for 1 minute, then add the tofu and stir well.

7 Pour in the stock and add the salt, sake or wine and mirin. Bring to a boil. Skim the broth and simmer for 5 minutes.

8 In a small bowl, dissolve the miso paste in a little of the soup, then return it to the pan. Simmer the soup for 10 minutes, until the vegetables are soft. Add the soy sauce, then remove from heat. Serve immediately in four bowls, garnished with the snowpeas.

COOK'S TIP
Konnyaku is a special cake made from flour that is produced from a root vegetable called devil's tongue. It has a subtle slightly fishy flavor.

BOILED FRIED TOFU WITH HIJIKI SEAWEED

oiled dishes, known as *nimono*, are enjoyed throughout the year in Japanese homes.

INGREDIENTS
³/₄ ounce dried hijiki seaweed
1 sheet Japanese fried tofu (aburage)
1¹/₄ ounces carrot
1¹/₄ ounces fresh shiitake mushrooms,
stems removed
1 tablespoon oil
generous ¹/₃ cup instant dashi
4¹/₂ teaspoons sake or dry white wine
1 tablespoon mirin
4¹/₂ teaspoons soy sauce
4¹/₂ teaspoons sugar

SERVES 4

1 Wash the hijiki seaweed and soak it in cold water for 30 minutes. Drain well. Do not soak for any longer, as it will lack flavor. During soaking, the hijiki will expand to about six times its dried volume.

2 Put the tofu in a strainer and rinse with hot water from a kettle to remove any excess oil. Shred it to 1¹/₄-inch lengths. Shred the carrot and shiitake mushrooms into strips of about the same size.

3 Heat the oil in a large pan. Add the carrot, stir once, then add the shiitake mushrooms and stir-fry over high heat for 1 minute. Add the hijiki, stir, then add the fried tofu and stir-fry for 1 minute.

4 Pour in the dashi, sake or wine, mirin and soy sauce. Stir in the sugar. Bring to a boil and reduce the heat, then simmer until all the soup has evaporated, stirring occasionally. Serve the tofu hot or cold, in four small bowls.

COOK'S TIP
Hijiki is a dried seaweed with a high fiber content. If Japanese fried tofu is not available, Chinese fried tofu may be used instead.

WINTER TOFU AND VEGETABLES

T his Japanese dish is brought bubbling hot to the table with a pot of dip to accompany the freshly cooked tofu and vegetables.

INGREDIENTS
1 sheet kombu seaweed, 8 x 4 inches
1 pound 5 ounces Japanese silken tofu,
4 x 3¹/₄ x 1¹/₄ inches
2 leeks
4 shiitake mushrooms, cross cut in top
and stems removed
scallions, to garnish

FOR THE DIP
scant 1 cup soy sauce
1 tablespoon mirin
generous ¹/₃ cup bonito flakes

SERVES 4

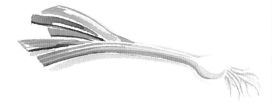

1 Half fill a large flameproof casserole or saucepan with cold water and soak the kombu seaweed in it for 30 minutes.

2 Cut the silken tofu into 1½-inch cubes. Slice the leeks diagonally into ¾-inch thick slices.

3 To make the dip, bring the soy sauce and mirin to a boil, then add the bonito flakes. Remove from heat and set aside until all the flakes have sunk to the bottom of the pan, then strain the sauce and pour it into a small heatproof basin.

4 Stand the basin in the middle of the pan, placing it on an upturned saucer, if necessary, so that it is well above the level of the water. This keeps the dip hot. Bring the water to a boil.

5 Add the mushrooms and leeks to the pan, and cook for about 5 minutes over medium heat, until softened. Then gently add the tofu. When the tofu starts floating, it is ready to eat. If the tofu won't all fit in the pan, it can be added during the meal.

6 Take the pan to the table and spoon the dip into four small bowls. Sprinkle the scallions into the dip. Diners help themselves to tofu and vegetables from the pan and eat them with the dip. The kombu seaweed is used only to flavor the dish; it is not eaten.

DEEP-FRIED TOFU AND ASPARAGUS IN STOCK

Agedashi is the name for dishes of deep-fried *(age)* ingredients served in a stock *(dashi)* or thin sauce. Here, deep-fried tofu and asparagus are served in a thin stock-based sauce and topped with tomato. A cup of sake goes very well with this *Agedashi*.

INGREDIENTS
7 ounces fresh Japanese tofu,
4 x 2 x 1¹/₄ inches
4 asparagus spears, trimmed of tough
stalk ends
1 tomato, skinned
oil, for deep-frying
cornstarch, for coating

FOR THE SAUCE
scant 1 cup instant dashi
¹/₄ cup mirin
¹/₄ cup soy sauce

SERVES 4

1 Wrap the tofu in a dish towel and press between two plates for 30 minutes, removing any excess moisture. Alternatively, wrap the tofu in paper towels, place it on a plate and cook it in the microwave for 1 minute . Cut the tofu into eight cubes, each measuring about 1 inch.

2 Cut the asparagus into 1¼–1½-inch lengths. Halve the tomato and remove the seeds, then cut it into ¼-inch cubes.

3 Slowly heat the oil for deep-frying to a temperature of 340°F. Coat the tofu with cornstarch.

4 Deep-fry the tofu pieces in two batches over medium heat, until golden, allowing 7–10 minutes to ensure that the tofu is cooked thoroughly. It starts to expand once it is cooked. Drain well. Keep the oil temperature at 340°F during cooking.

5 Meanwhile, place the ingredients for the sauce in a saucepan and bring to a boil, then simmer gently for 3 minutes. Deep-fry the asparagus lengths for 2 minutes and drain them well.

6 Place the tofu on a large plate and arrange the asparagus on top. Pour on the hot sauce and sprinkle the tomato on top. Serve immediately.

Rice paddies are part of the topography of China, Japan, Indonesia and Vietnam, visible from the air while flying overhead. Rice is the staple of any Asian meal and there are many varieties to complement different types of food. Coconut Rice from Thailand uses delicate and aromatic jasmine rice. Basmati rice, another fragrant variety from the foothills of the Himalayas, makes delicious pilafs that are full of spices and nuts.

Noodles are also popular throughout Asia. There is much speculation about whether the Chinese invented noodles before the Italians started producing spaghetti. One theory is that Marco Polo brought the secret of pasta-making back to Italy after his 13th-century journey across China.

Thai Fried Noodles is considered one of the national dishes of Thailand and features a rich mixture of rice noodles, vegetables and seafood. Egg noodles are more common in Chinese cooking, while Japanese dishes also call for rice, buckwheat and cellophane noodles.

QUICK BASMATI AND NUT PILAF

Light and fragrant basmati rice from the foothills of the Himalayas cooks perfectly using this simple pilaf method. Use your favorite nuts—even unsalted peanuts are good, although almonds or cashews are more exotic, and pistachios add color and flavor.

INGREDIENTS
1¼ cups basmati rice
1–2 tablespoons sunflower oil
1 onion, chopped
1 garlic clove, crushed
1 large carrot, coarsely grated
1 teaspoon cumin seeds
2 teaspoons ground cilantro
2 teaspoons black mustard seeds
(optional)
4 cardamom pods
1 bay leaf
2 cups chicken or vegetable stock or water
½ cup unsalted nuts
salt and ground black pepper
chopped cilantro and cilantro sprig,
to garnish

SERVES 4–6

1 Put the rice in a sieve and wash under cold running water. Transfer the rice to a bowl, add fresh water and soak for about 30 minutes. Drain thoroughly in a sieve.

2 Heat the oil in a large shallow pan, add the onion, garlic and carrot and cook gently for about 5 minutes. Add the rice to the pan with the cumin seeds, ground cilantro, black mustard seeds, if using, cardamom pods and bay leaf. Cook for another 1–2 minutes, stirring the rice and spices, until the rice is thoroughly coated with the spice mixture.

3 Pour in the chicken or vegetable stock or water, and season well. Bring to a boil, cover, lower the heat and simmer very gently for about 10 minutes.

4 Remove the pan from heat without lifting the lid—this helps the rice firm up. Let stand for about 5 minutes, until small steam holes appear in the center. Discard the cardamom pods and bay leaf.

5 Stir in the nuts and check the seasoning. Sprinkle with chopped cilantro and add a cilantro sprig, to garnish.

COLORFUL PULLAO RICE

This lightly spiced rice makes a very attractive accompaniment to many Indian dishes.

INGREDIENTS
2 cups basmati rice
6 tablespoons unsalted butter
4 cloves
4 green cardamom pods
2 bay leaves
1 teaspoon salt
4 cups water
few drops each of yellow, green and red
food coloring

SERVES 4–6

1 Wash the rice twice to remove any grit, drain and set aside in a bowl.

2 Melt the butter in a saucepan, then add the cloves, cardamoms, bay leaves and salt. Lower the heat and add the rice. Fry for about 1 minute, stirring constantly. Add the water and bring to a boil. As soon as it has boiled, cover the pan and reduce the heat. Cook for 15–20 minutes.

3 Just before serving, pour a few drops of each food coloring into different parts of the pan. Let stand, covered, for 5 minutes, mix gently and serve.

FRUITY PULLAO

This is a lovely way to cook rice that goes very well with all meat dishes, especially lamb.

INGREDIENTS
2 cups basmati rice
6 tablespoons unsalted butter
1 tablespoon corn oil
2 bay leaves
6 black peppercorns
4 green cardamom pods
1 teaspoon salt
½ cup golden raisins
½ cup sliced almonds
4 cups water

SERVES 4–6

COOK'S TIP
Turmeric colors rice yellow. Add
¼–½ teaspoon to the boiling water
before adding the rice.

---

1 Wash the rice twice to remove any grit, drain and set aside in a sieve while you prepare and cook the spices.

2 Heat the butter with the oil in a saucepan. Lower the heat and add the bay leaves, peppercorns and cardamom pods, and fry for about 30 seconds.

3 Add the rice, salt, golden raisins and sliced almonds, stir-fry for about 1 minute, then pour in the water. Bring to a boil, then cover with a tightly-fitting lid and lower the heat. Cook for 15–20 minutes.

4 Turn off the heat and lrt the rice stand, still covered, for about 5 minutes before serving.

OPPOSITE: Colorful Pullao Rice (TOP) and Fruity Pullao

SAFFRON AND CARDAMOM RICE

There are two main ways of cooking rice: one in which all the water is absorbed by the rice and the other where the surplus water is drained, getting rid of any starch from the rice. This recipe uses the second method. Try serving this with Spiced Okra with Almonds.

INGREDIENTS

2⅔ cups basmati rice
3 cups water
3 green cardamom pods
2 cloves
1 teaspoon salt
½ teaspoon crushed saffron threads
3 tablespoons low-fat milk

SERVES 6

1 Wash the rice at least twice and place it in a saucepan with the water. Add the cardamon, cloves and salt to the saucepan. Bring to a boil, cover, lower the heat and simmer for about 10 minutes.

2 Meanwhile, place the saffron and milk in a small pan and warm. (Alternatively, put the saffron and milk in a cup and warm for 1 minute in a microwave.)

3 To test whether the rice is ready, use a slotted spoon to lift out a few grains and press them between your index finger and thumb. They should feel soft on the outside but still a little hard in the middle. If the rice is ready, remove the pan from heat, and carefully drain the rice through a sieve. Rinse out the pan.

4 Return the rice to the pan and pour the saffron and milk on top. Cover with a tight-fitting lid and place the pan over medium heat for 7–10 minutes.

5 Remove the pan from heat and let the rice stand, still covered, for another 5 minutes before serving.

TOMATO RICE

his spicy Indian dish can be served as a side dish or light supper. It goes well with fish.

INGREDIENTS
2 tablespoons corn oil
½ teaspoon onion seeds
1 onion, sliced
2 tomatoes, peeled and sliced
1 orange or yellow bell pepper, seeded and sliced
1 teaspoon grated fresh ginger root
1 garlic clove, crushed
1 teaspoon chili powder
2 tablespoons chopped cilantro
1 potato, diced
1½ teaspoons salt
⅓ cup frozen peas
2⅓ cups basmati rice, washed
3 cups water

SERVES 4

1 Heat the oil in a large saucepan and fry the onion seeds for about 30 seconds. Add the sliced onion and sauté gently for about 5 minutes until softened.

2 Gradually add the tomatoes, pepper, ginger, garlic, chili powder, cilantro, potato, salt and peas, and stir-fry over medium heat for 5 minutes.

3 Add the rice and stir for about 1 minute, then pour in the water and bring to a boil. Lower the heat to medium, cover and cook for 12–15 minutes. Let the rice stand, covered, for 5 minutes before serving.

COOK'S TIP
Rice should be cooked in a pan with a tight-fitting lid. This prevents any steam from escaping and ensures that the rice cooks evenly.

COCONUT RICE

 his dish is usually served with a tangy papaya salad to balance the richness of the coconut.

INGREDIENTS
2 cups jasmine rice
1 cup water
2 cups coconut milk
½ teaspoon salt
2 tablespoons sugar
fresh shredded coconut, to garnish (optional)

SERVES 4–6

1 Wash the rice in several changes of cold water until it runs clear. Place the water, coconut milk, salt and sugar in a heavy saucepan.

2 Add the rice, cover and bring to a boil. Reduce the heat to low and simmer for 15–20 minutes or until the rice is tender to the bite and cooked through.

3 Turn off the heat and allow the rice to rest in the pan for 5–10 minutes.

4 Fluff up the rice with chopsticks before serving. Garnish, if desired, with fresh shredded coconut.

PINEAPPLE FRIED RICE

W hen buying a pineapple, look for a sweet-smelling fruit with an even brownish/yellow skin. To test for ripeness, tap the base—a dull sound indicates that the fruit is ripe. The flesh should also give slightly when pressed.

INGREDIENTS
1 pineapple
2 tablespoons vegetable oil
1 small onion, finely chopped
2 green chiles, seeded and chopped
8 ounces lean pork,
cut into small dice
4 ounces cooked shelled shrimp
3–4 cups cold cooked rice
2 ounces roasted cashews
2 scallions, chopped
2 tablespoons fish sauce
1 tablespoon soy sauce
2 red chiles and 1 green chile, sliced, and
10–12 mint leaves, to garnish

SERVES 4–6

1 Cut the pineapple in half lengthwise and remove the flesh from both halves by cutting around inside the skin. Reserve the skin shells. You need 4 ounces of fruit, chopped finely (keep the rest for a dessert).

COOK'S TIP
This dish is ideal to prepare for a special-occasion meal. Served in the pineapple skin shells, it is sure to be the focal point of the dinner.

2 Heat the oil in a wok or large frying pan. Add the onion and chiles and cook for 3–5 minutes, until softened. Add the pork and cook until it is brown on all sides.

3 Stir in the shrimp and rice and toss well together. Continue to stir-fry until the rice is thoroughly heated. Add the chopped pineapple, cashews and scallions. Season with fish sauce and soy sauce.

4 Spoon into the pineapple skin shells. Garnish with red and green chiles and shredded mint leaves.

THAI FRIED NOODLES

Phat (Pad) Thai has a fascinating flavor and texture. It is made with rice noodles and is considered one of the national dishes of Thailand.

INGREDIENTS

12 ounces rice noodles
3 tablespoons vegetable oil
1 tablespoon chopped garlic
16 uncooked king shrimp, shelled, tails
left intact and deveined
2 eggs, lightly beaten
1 tablespoon dried shrimp, rinsed
2 tablespoons pickled white radish
2 ounces fried tofu, cut into
small slivers
½ teaspoon dried chile flakes
4 ounces garlic chives,
cut into 2-inch lengths
8 ounces bean sprouts
2 ounces roasted peanuts,
coarsely ground
1 teaspoon sugar
1 tablespoon dark soy sauce
2 tablespoons fish sauce
2 tablespoons tamarind juice
2 tablespoons cilantro leaves and 1 kaffir
lime cut into wedges, to garnish

SERVES 4–6

1 Soak the noodles in warm water for 20–30 minutes, then drain.

2 Heat 1 tablespoon of the oil in a wok or large frying pan. Add the garlic and fry until golden. Stir in the shrimp and cook for 1–2 minutes until pink, tossing occasionally. Remove and set aside.

3 Heat another 1 tablespoon of oil in the wok. Add the eggs and tilt the wok to spread them into a thin sheet. Stir to scramble and break the egg into small pieces. Remove from the wok and set aside with the shrimp.

4 Heat the remaining oil in the same wok. Add the dried shrimp, pickled white radish, fried tofu and dried chile flakes. Stir briefly. Add the soaked noodles and stir-fry for 5 minutes.

5 Add the garlic chives, half the bean-sprouts and half the ground peanuts. Season with the sugar, soy sauce, fish sauce and tamarind juice. Mix well and cook until the noodles are heated through.

6 Return the shrimp and egg mixture to the wok and mix with the noodles. Serve garnished with the rest of the bean sprouts, peanuts, cilantro leaves and lime wedges.

CHIANG MAI NOODLE SOUP

A signature dish of the city of Chiang Mai, this delicious noodle soup has Burmese origins and is the Thai equivalent of the Malaysian "Laksa."

INGREDIENTS
2½ cups coconut milk
2 tablespoons red curry paste
1 teaspoon ground turmeric
1 pound chicken thighs, boned and cut into bite-size chunks
2½ cups chicken stock
¼ cup fish sauce
1 tablespoon dark soy sauce
juice of ½–1 lime
1 pound fresh egg noodles, blanched briefly in boiling water
salt and freshly ground black pepper

FOR THE GARNISH
3 scallions, chopped
4 red chiles, seeded and chopped
4 shallots, chopped
4 tablespoons sliced pickled mustard leaves, rinsed
2 tablespoons fried sliced garlic
cilantro leaves
4 fried noodle nests (optional)

SERVES 4–6

1 Put one third of the coconut milk into a large saucepan, bring to a boil and stir with a wooden spoon until it separates.

2 Add the curry paste and ground turmeric, stir to mix completely and cook until fragrant.

3 Add the chicken and stir-fry for about 2 minutes, ensuring that all the chunks are coated with the paste.

4 Add the remaining coconut milk, chicken stock, fish sauce and soy sauce. Season with salt and freshly ground black pepper to taste. Simmer gently for 7–10 minutes. Remove from heat and stir in the lime juice.

5 Reheat the noodles in boiling water, drain and divide between individual bowls. Divide the chicken between the bowls and ladle in the hot soup. Top each serving with a few of each of the garnishes.

INDONESIAN PORK AND SHRIMP RICE

N*asi Goreng* is one of the most familiar and well-loved Indonesian dishes. It is a great way to use up leftover rice, chicken and other meats such as pork. It is important that the rice is cold and the grains are separated before adding the other ingredients, so it is best to cook the rice the day before.

INGREDIENTS

1½ cups long-grain rice, such as basmati,
cooked and left until cold
2 eggs
2 tablespoons water
7 tablespoons oil
8 ounces pork fillet or fillet of beef
4 ounces cooked, peeled shrimp
6–8 ounces cooked
chicken, chopped
2–3 fresh red chiles, seeded and sliced
½-inch cube terasi
2 garlic cloves, crushed
1 onion, sliced
2 tablespoons dark soy sauce or
3–4 tablespoons ketchup
salt and freshly ground black pepper
celery leaves, deep-fried onions and
cilantro sprigs, to garnish

SERVES 4–6

1 Cook and cool the rice. Fork it through to separate the grains and keep it in a covered pan or dish until required.

2 Beat the eggs. Add the seasoning and water and make two or three omelets in a frying pan, with a small amount of oil. Roll up each omelet, let cool, and cut in strips when cold. Set aside.

3 Cut the pork or beef into neat strips and put the meat, shrimp and chicken pieces into separate bowls. Shred one of the chiles and reserve it.

4 Put the *terasi*, with the remaining chile, garlic and onion in a food processor and grind to a fine paste. Alternatively, pound together using a mortar and pestle.

5 Fry the paste in the remaining hot oil, without browning, until it gives off a rich, spicy aroma, for about 3 minutes. Add the pork or beef, tossing the meat constantly, to seal in the juices. Cook for 2 minutes, stirring constantly.

6 Add the shrimp, cook for another 2 minutes, and then stir in the chicken, cold rice, dark soy sauce or ketchup and season to taste. Stir constantly to keep the rice light and fluffy and prevent it from sticking to the pan.

7 Turn the rice mixture onto a hot platter and garnish with the omelet strips, celery leaves, deep-fried onions, reserved shredded chile and the fresh, chopped cilantro sprigs.

EGG FRIED NOODLES

Yellow bean sauce gives these noodles a savory flavor. They are eaten all over Asia, accompanying many meat and vegetable dishes.

INGREDIENTS

12 ounces medium-thick egg noodles
4 tablespoons vegetable oil
4 scallions, cut into
½-inch rounds
juice of 1 lime
1 tablespoon soy sauce
2 garlic cloves, finely chopped
6 ounces skinless, boneless chicken
breast, sliced
6 ounces raw shrimp,
peeled and deveined
6 ounces squid, cleaned
and cut into rings
1 tablespoon yellow bean sauce
1 tablespoon fish sauce
1 tablespoon light brown sugar
2 eggs
cilantro leaves, to garnish

SERVES 4–6

1 Cook the noodles in a saucepan of boiling water until just tender, then drain well and set aside.

2 Heat half the oil in a wok or large frying pan. Add the scallions, stir-fry for 2 minutes, then add the noodles, lime juice and soy sauce and stir-fry for another 2–3 minutes. Transfer the mixture to a bowl, cover, and keep warm.

3 Heat the remaining oil in the wok or pan. Add the garlic, chicken, shrimp and squid. Stir-fry over high heat for about 5 minutes or until all the ingredients are cooked through.

4 Stir in the yellow bean sauce, fish sauce and sugar, then break the eggs into the mixture, one at a time, stirring gently until they set.

5 Add the noodles to the wok or pan. Mix all the ingredients together well, and heat through. Serve garnished with cilantro leaves.

SOFT FRIED NOODLES

his basic, traditional dish is an ideal accompaniment for rich or spicy main courses.

INGREDIENTS

11 ounces dried egg noodles
2 tablespoons vegetable oil
2 tablespoons finely chopped scallions
soy sauce, to taste
salt and freshly ground black pepper
chopped scallion, to garnish
deep-fried onion rings, to serve

SERVES 4–6

1 Cook the noodles in a large saucepan of boiling water until just tender, following the directions on the package. Drain, rinse under cold running water to remove any excess starch, and drain again thoroughly.

2 Heat the oil in a wok and swirl it around. Add the scallions and cook for about 30 seconds. Add the noodles, stirring gently to separate the strands.

3 Reduce the heat and fry the noodles, until they are lightly browned and crisp on the outside, but still soft on the inside.

4 Season with soy sauce, salt and freshly ground black pepper. Garnish with chopped scallions and serve immetiately with deep-fried onion rings.

SEAFOOD CHOW MEIN

Chow mein is a Chinese-American dish in which seafood, chicken and vegetables are cooked separately and then combined with stir-fried noodles. This basic recipe can be adapted according to taste, using different items for the "dressing."

INGREDIENTS

3 ounces squid, cleaned

3 ounces raw shrimp

3–4 fresh scallops

½ egg white

1 tablespoon cornstarch, mixed with a little water

9 ounces egg noodles

5–6 tablespoons vegetable oil

2 ounces snowpeas

½ teaspoon salt

½ teaspoon light brown sugar

1 tablespoon Chinese rice wine or dry sherry

2 tablespoons light soy sauce

2 scallions, finely sliced

chicken stock, if necessary

few drops of sesame oil

SERVES 4

1 Open up the squid and score the inside in a criss-cross pattern. Cut the squid into ½–1-inch pieces and soak in boiling water until all the pieces curl up. Rinse in cold water and drain.

2 Peel the shrimp and cut each in half lengthwise. Cut each scallop into 3 thin slices. Mix the scallops and shrimp with the egg white and cornstarch paste.

3 Cook the noodles in boiling water according to the manufacturer's instructions, then drain and rinse under cold water. Mix with about 1 tablespoon of the oil.

4 Heat 2–3 tablespoons of the oil in a wok until hot. Stir-fry the snowpeas and seafood for about 2 minutes, then add the salt, sugar, wine or sherry, half of the soy sauce and the sliced scallions. Stir the mixture and add a little stock if necessary. Remove and keep warm.

5 Heat the remaining oil in the wok and stir-fry the noodles for 2–3 minutes with the remaining soy sauce. Place the noodles in a large serving dish and arrange the seafood mixture on them. Sprinkle with a few drops of sesame oil. Either serve immediately or, if desired, when cold.

SPECIAL CHOW MEIN

L ap cheong is a special air-dried Chinese sausage. It is available at most Chinese supermarkets. If you cannot buy it, substitute for diced ham, chorizo or salami.

INGREDIENTS

3 tablespoons vegetable oil
2 garlic cloves, sliced
1 teaspoon chopped ginger
2 red chiles, chopped
2 lap cheong, about 3 ounces, rinsed and
sliced (optional)
1 boneless chicken breast, thinly sliced
16 uncooked jumbo shrimp, shelled, tails
left intact and deveined
4 ounces green beans
8 ounces bean sprouts
2 ounces garlic chives
1 pound egg noodles, cooked in boiling
water until tender
2 tablespoons soy sauce
1 tablespoon oyster sauce
1 tablespoon sesame oil
salt and freshly ground black pepper
2 scallions, shredded, and
1 tablespoon cilantro leaves,
to garnish

SERVES 4–6

1 Heat 1 tablespoon of the oil in a wok or large frying pan and fry the garlic, ginger and chiles. Add the lap cheong (or its substitute), chicken, shrimp and beans. Stir-fry for about 2 minutes over high heat or until the chicken and shrimp are cooked. Transfer the mixture to a bowl and set aside.

2 Heat the rest of the oil in the same wok. Add the bean sprouts and garlic chives. Stir-fry for 1–2 minutes.

3 Add the noodles and toss and stir to mix. Season with soy sauce, oyster sauce, salt and pepper.

4 Return the shrimp mixture to the wok. Reheat and mix well with the noodles. Stir in the sesame oil. Serve garnished with scallions and cilantro leaves.

NOODLES WITH VEGETABLES

This Chinese dish makes a delicious vegetarian supper on its own, or serve it as a side dish with a main course of fish, meat or poultry.

INGREDIENTS
8 ounces egg noodles
1 tablespoon sesame oil
3 tablespoons peanut oil
2 garlic cloves, thinly sliced
1-inch piece fresh ginger root, finely chopped
2 fresh red chiles, seeded and sliced
4 ounces broccoli, broken into small florets
4 ounces baby corn
6 ounces shiitake or oyster mushrooms, sliced
1 bunch scallions, sliced
4 ounces bok choy or Chinese cabbage, shredded
4 ounces bean sprouts
1–2 tablespoons dark soy sauce
salt and ground black pepper

SERVES 4

1 Cook the egg noodles in a pan of boiling salted water according to the manufacturer's instructions. Drain well and toss in the sesame oil. Set aside.

2 Heat the peanut oil in a wok or large frying pan and stir-fry the garlic and ginger for 1 minute. Add the chiles, broccoli, baby corn and mushrooms and stir-fry for another 2 minutes.

3 Add the sliced scallions, shredded bok choy or cabbage and the bean sprouts to the wok. Stir-fry for about 2 minutes.

4 Toss in the noodles, soy sauce and black pepper. Continue to cook over high heat for 2–3 minutes, until the ingredients are well mixed and warmed. Serve immediately.

SWEET-AND-SOUR NOODLES

N oodles combined with chicken and a selection of vegetables in a tasty sweet-and-sour sauce create a quick and satisfying meal.

INGREDIENTS
10 ounces egg noodles
2 tablespoons vegetable oil
3 scallions, chopped
1 garlic clove, crushed
1-inch piece fresh ginger root, peeled and grated
1 teaspoon hot paprika
1 teaspoon ground cilantro
3 boneless chicken breasts, sliced
4 ounces snowpeas, trimmed
4 ounces baby corn
8 ounces fresh bean sprouts
1 tablespoon cornstarch
3 tablespoons soy sauce
3 tablespoons lemon juice
1 tablespoon sugar
3 tablespoons chopped cilantro or scallion tops, to garnish

SERVES 4

1 Bring a large saucepan of salted water to a boil. Add the noodles and cook according to the manufacturer's instructions. Drain, cover and keep warm.

2 Heat the oil in a wok or large frying pan. Add the scallions and cook over low heat. Mix in the garlic, ginger, paprika, ground cilantro and chicken, then stir-fry for 3–4 minutes. Add the snowpeas, baby corn and bean sprouts and steam briefly. Then stir in the cooked noodles.

3 Combine the cornstarch, soy sauce, lemon juice and sugar in a small bowl. Add to the wok and simmer briefly to thicken. Serve garnished with chopped cilantro or scallion tops.

MIXED RICE

Rice is a staple part of the Japanese diet, and this is one of the many ways of cooking it. This recipe makes a very good party dish, and you can add a variety of ingredients to create your own special version. *Aburage*, a deep-fried tofu, is sold ready-made at Japanese stores.

INGREDIENTS

6 dried shiitake mushrooms
2 sheets fried tofu (aburage), *each*
5 x 2½ inches
6 snowpeas
1 carrot, cut into matchstick strips
4 ounces chicken fillet, diced
2 tablespoons sugar
7½ teaspoons soy sauce
salt
7 cups freshly boiled
Japanese rice

SERVES 4

1 Soak the dried shiitake mushrooms in 3½ cups water for about 30 minutes. Place a small plate or saucer on top of the mushrooms to keep them submerged during soaking.

2 Put the fried tofu into a strainer and pour in hot water from a kettle to remove any excess fat. Squeeze the tofu and cut it in half lengthwise, then slice it into ¼-inch wide strips.

3 Boil the snowpeas, then drain and refresh them in cold water. Drain well. Shred the snowpeas finely.

4 Drain the shiitake mushrooms, reserving the soaking water, and carefully remove their stems. Using a sharp knife, finely slice the mushroom caps. Pour the soaking water into a saucepan and add the tofu, carrots, chicken and shiitake mushrooms.

5 Bring the ingredients to a boil, then skim the broth and simmer for 1–2 minutes. Add the sugar and cook for 1 minute, then add the soy sauce and salt. Simmer gently until most of the liquid has evaporated, leaving only a small amount of concentrated broth.

6 Mix in a boiled hot rice, sprinkle the snowpeas on top and serve the mixed rice immediately.

CHILLED NOODLES

These classic Japanese cold noodles are known as *somen*. The noodles are surprisingly refreshing when eaten with the accompanying ingredients and a delicately flavored dip. The noodles are served with ice to ensure that they remain chilled until they are eaten.

INGREDIENTS
oil, for cooking
2 small eggs, beaten with a pinch of salt
1 sheet yaki-nori *seaweed, finely shredded*
¹/₂ bunch of scallions, sliced
4 teaspoons wasabi paste
14 ounces dried somen *noodles*
ice cubes, to serve

FOR THE DIP
4 cups kombu and bonito stock
or instant dashi
scant 1 cup soy sauce
1 tablespoon mirin

SERVES 4

1 Prepare the dip in advance so that it has time to chill. Bring the ingredients to a boil, then chill thoroughly.

2 Heat a little oil in a frying pan. Pour in half the beaten eggs, tilting the pan to coat the bottom evenly. Let the egg set, then turn it over and cook the second side briefly. Turn the omelet out onto a board. Cook the remaining egg in the same way.

3 Leave the omelets to cool, and then shred them finely. Divide the shredded omelet, *yaki-nori*, scallions and wasabi between four small bowls.

4 Boil the *somen* noodles according to the package instructions and drain. Rinse the noodles in or under cold running water, stirring with chopsticks, then drain well.

5 Place the cooked noodles on a large plate and add some ice cubes on top to keep them cool.

6 Pour the cold dip into four more small bowls. The noodles and the selected accompaniments should be dipped into the chilled dip before they are eaten.

FIVE-FLAVOR NOODLES

 The Japanese title for this dish is *Gomoku Yakisoba*, meaning five different ingredients.

INGREDIENTS
*11 ounces dried Chinese thin egg noodles
or 1¹/₄ pounds fresh* yakisoba *noodles
7 ounces lean boneless pork, thinly sliced
4¹/₂ teaspoons oil
¹/₄ ounce fresh ginger root, grated
1 garlic clove, crushed
1³/₄ cups green cabbage, roughly chopped
¹/₂ cup bean sprouts
1 green bell pepper, seeded and cut into
fine strips
1 red bell pepper, seeded and cut into
fine strips
salt and white pepper
4 teaspoons* ao-nori *seaweed,
to garnish (optional)*

FOR THE SEASONING
*¹/₄ cup Worcestershire sauce
1 tablespoon soy sauce
1 tablespoon oyster sauce
1 tablespoon sugar
¹/₂ teaspoon salt*

SERVES 4

1 Boil the noodles according to the package instructions and drain. Cut the pork into 1¹/₄–1¹/₂-inch strips and season with salt and white pepper.

2 Heat 1¹/₂ teaspoons oil in a large frying pan or a wok and stir-fry the pork until just cooked, then remove it from the pan.

3 Wipe the pan with paper towels, and then heat the remaining oil in it. Add the ginger, garlic and cabbage and stir-fry for 1 minute.

4 Add the bean sprouts and stir until softened, then add the green and red peppers and stir-fry for 1 minute.

5 Replace the pork in the pan and add the noodles. Stir in all the seasoning ingredients and more white pepper if desired. Stir-fry for 2–3 minutes.

6 Serve immediately, sprinkled with the *ao-nori* seaweed, if desired.

INDIVIDUAL NOODLE CASSEROLES

Traditionally, these individual casseroles are cooked in separate earthenware pots. *Nabe* means pot and *yaki* means to heat, providing the Japanese title of *Nabeyaki Udon* for this exciting recipe.

INGREDIENTS
4 ounces boneless chicken thigh
¹/₂ teaspoon salt
¹/₂ teaspoon sake or dry white wine
¹/₂ teaspoon soy sauce
1 leek
4 ounces whole spinach, trimmed
11 ounces dried udon *noodles*
or 1¹/₄ pounds fresh
4 shiitake mushrooms, stems removed
4 size 4 eggs
seven-flavor spice, to serve (optional)

FOR THE SOUP
6 cups instant dashi
4¹/₂ teaspoons soy sauce
1¹/₃ teaspoons salt
1 tablespoon mirin

SERVES 4

1 Cut the chicken thigh into small chunks and sprinkle with the salt, sake or wine and soy sauce. Cut the leek diagonally into 1³/₄-inch slices.

2 Boil the spinach for 2 minutes. Drain and soak in cold water for 1 minute. Drain, squeeze and cut into 1¹/₂-inch lengths.

3 Boil the dried *udon* noodles according to the package instructions, but for 3 minutes less than the suggested cooking time. If using fresh *udon* noodles, place them in boiling water, disentangle the noodles well and then drain them.

COOK'S TIP
Always use hot rice to make these balls, then let them cool before wrapping each one in plastic wrap.

4 Bring the ingredients for the soup to a boil in a saucepan and add the chicken and leeks. Skim the broth, then cook it for 5 minutes.

5 Divide the *udon* noodles between four individual flameproof casseroles. Pour the soup, chicken and leeks into the casseroles. Place over medium heat, then add the shiitake mushrooms.

6 Gently break an egg into each casserole. Cover and simmer for 2 minutes. Divide the spinach among the casseroles and simmer for 1 minute.

7 Serve immediately, standing the hot casseroles on plates or table mats. Sprinkle seven-flavor spice on the casseroles, if desired.

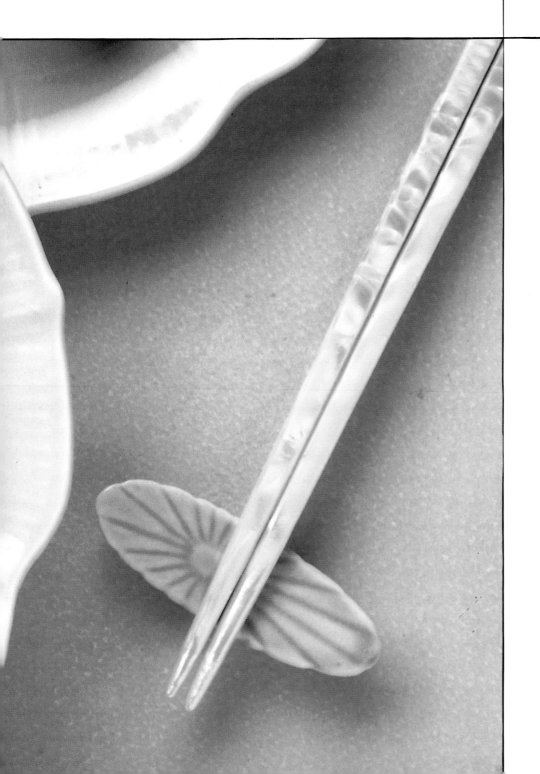

DESSERTS

After most Asian meals, dessert consists of different types of fruit, simply prepared. In India or Thailand, delicious mangoes may be prepared in sorbets or ice creams. In China the ubiquitous toffee apple is a popular dessert along with lychees and pineapples.

Indians, however, are known for having a sweet tooth and Kulfi, the frozen dessert made from evaporated milk, nuts and rose-water, is a favorite treat. Not surprisingly from countries that eat so much rice and pasta, these ingredients also figure highly in puddings, with additions such as coconut milk in Thailand and saffron and pistachios in India. Chinese desserts feature sweetened red bean paste, used in pancakes, along with some other very unusual and delicious dishes, well worth trying.

KULFI

In India *kulfi-wallahs* (ice cream vendors) have always made *kulfi*, and continue to this day, without using modern freezers. *Kulfi* is packed into metal cones sealed with dough and then churned in clay pots until set. This method works extremely well in an ordinary freezer.

INGREDIENTS

3, 14-fluid ounce cans evaporated milk
3 egg whites, whisked until peaks form
2¼ cups confectioners' sugar
1 teaspoon ground cardamom
1 tablespoon rose water
1½ cups pistachios, chopped
½ cup golden raisins
¾ cup sliced almonds
8 candied cherries, halved

SERVES 4–6

1 Lie the cans of evaporated milk in one or two heavy-based pans with tight-fitting lids. Fill the pan with water to reach three-quarters of the way up the cans. Bring to the boil, cover the pan, and simmer for about 20 minutes. Alternatively, empty the milk into a pan and simmer for 20 minutes When cool, remove from the pan and chill for 24 hours.

2 Open the cans and pour the evaporated milk into a large chilled bowl. Whisk until it doubles in volume, then fold in the whisked egg whites and the confectioners' sugar.

3 Gently fold in the cardamom, rose water, pistachios, golden raisins, almonds and candied cherries. Cover the bowl with plastic wrap and put in the freezer for 1 hour.

4 Remove the ice cream from the freezer and mix well with a fork to break up any ice crystals that have formed around the edge. Transfer to a freezer container and return to the freezer to freeze completely. Remove the ice cream from the freezer 10 minutes before serving to soften a little. Scoop into a chilled bowl to serve.

ORANGES WITH SAFFRON YOGURT

A fter a hot, spicy curry, a popular Indian dessert is simply sliced, juicy oranges sprinkled with a little cinnamon and served with a spoonful of saffron-flavored yogurt.

INGREDIENTS
4 large oranges
¼ teaspoon ground cinnamon
⅔ cup plain yogurt
2 teaspoons sugar
3–4 saffron threads
¼ teaspoon ground ginger
1 tablespoon chopped pistachios, toasted
fresh lemon balm or mint
sprigs, to decorate

SERVES 4

1 Slice the bottoms off the oranges so they sit upright on a board. Working from the top of the oranges, cut across the top and down one side. Follow the contours of the orange to reveal the orange flesh beneath the pith. Repeat until all the zest and pith has been removed, reserving any juice.

COOK'S TIP
Instead of ordinary oranges, try using clementines or blood oranges.

2 Slice the oranges thinly and remove any seeds. Place the oranges in a single layer, overlapping the slices, on a shallow serving platter. Sprinkle on the ground cinnamon, then cover and chill until you are ready to serve the dessert.

3 Combine the yogurt, sugar, saffron and ginger in a bowl and let stand for 5 minutes. Spoon into a serving bowl and sprinkle with the nuts. Spoon a little of the yogurt mixture onto each serving and decorate with lemon balm or mint sprigs.

LASSI

L assi is a very popular drink both in India and Pakistan. It is available at both roadside cafes and good hotels. There is no substitute for this drink, especially on a hot day. It is ideal served with hot dishes, as it helps the body to digest spicy food.

INGREDIENTS
1¼ cups plain yogurt
1 teaspoon sugar or to taste
1¼ cups ice water
2 tablespoons puréed fruit (optional)
1 tablespoon crushed pistachios

SERVES 4

COOK'S TIP
Fruit purée provides a filling, refreshing addition to traditional lassi. Try using strawberries, raspberries, mangoes and oranges—either fresh or frozen.

1 Place the yogurt in a bowl or pitcher and whisk it for about 2 minutes until frothy. Add the sugar to taste.

2 Pour in the water and the puréed fruit, if using, and continue to whisk for about 2 minutes.

3 Pour the lassi into tall serving glasses. Serve chilled, decorated with crushed pistachios.

MANGO SORBET WITH MANGO SAUCE

After a spicy meal, this makes a most refreshing dessert. Mango is said to be one of the most ancient fruits cultivated in India, having been brought by the god Shiva for his wife, Parvati.

INGREDIENTS
2 pounds mango pulp
½ teaspoon lemon juice
grated zest of 1 orange and 1 lime
4 egg whites, whisked until peaks form
¼ cup sugar
½ cup heavy cream
⅓ cup confectioners' sugar

SERVES 4–6

COOK'S TIP
To prepare mango pulp, cut each mango lengthwise on both sides of the pit, then slice the remaining mango from the pit. Make a lattice of cuts through each piece, cutting through the flesh but not the skin. Press the skin, so that the mango looks like a hedgehog, then cut the flesh from the skin. Purée in a blender.

1 In a large chilled bowl, mix 15 ounces of the mango pulp with the lemon juice and the orange and lime zest.

2 Gently fold in the egg whites and sugar. Cover with plastic wrap and place in the freezer for at least 1 hour.

3 Remove the mango mixture from the freezer and beat thoroughly. Transfer to a freezer and freeze fully.

4 To make the sauce, whip the cream with the confectioners' sugar and the remaining mango pulp. Cover and chill the sauce for 24 hours. Remove the sorbet from the freezer 10 minutes before serving so that it softens slightly. Using a spoon or ice cream scoop, transfer individual servings to chilled bowls and top each with a generous helping of mango sauce.

VERMICELLI PUDDING

Indian vermicelli, made from wheat, has a much finer texture than the Italian variety. It is readily available at Asian food stores as *seviyan*.

INGREDIENTS
4 ounces fine vermicelli
5 cups water
½ teaspoon saffron threads
1 tablespoon sugar
1 tablespoon each shredded fresh coconut or dry, shredded coconut, sliced almonds, chopped pistachios and sugar, to decorate
¼ cup fromage frais, to serve (optional)

SERVES 4

1 Crush the vermicelli in your hands and place in a saucepan. Pour in the water, add the saffron and bring to a boil. Boil for about 5 minutes.

2 Stir in the sugar and continue cooking until the water has evaporated from the vermicelli. Strain through a sieve, if necessary, to remove any excess liquid.

3 Ladle the vermicelli into a serving dish and decorate with the coconut, almonds, chopped pistachios and sugar. Serve with fromage frais, if desired.

THAI-STYLE BAKED RICE PUDDING

Black glutinous rice, also known as black sticky rice, has long black grains and a nutty taste similar to wild rice. This baked pudding has a distinct character and flavor all of its own.

INGREDIENTS

6 ounces white or black glutinous (sticky) rice
2 tablespoons light brown sugar
2 cups coconut milk
1 cup water
3 eggs
2 tablespoons sugar
confectioners' sugar, to decorate

SERVES 4–6

1 Combine the glutinous rice, brown sugar, half the coconut milk and all the water in a medium-size saucepan.

2 Bring to a boil and simmer for 15–20 minutes or until the rice has absorbed most of the liquid, stirring occasionally. Preheat the oven to 300°F.

3 Transfer all of the rice into one large ovenproof dish or divide it evenly between individual ramekins. Then combine the eggs, remaining coconut milk and sugar in a bowl.

4 Strain the mixture and pour evenly over the rice.

5 Place the dish in a baking pan. Pour in enough boiling water to come halfway up the sides of the dish.

6 Cover the dish with a piece of aluminum foil and bake for about 35 minutes to 1 hour or until the custard is set. Serve warm or cold, sprinkled with confectioners' sugar.

MANGO ICE CREAM

Mangoes are used widely in Asian cooking, particularly in Thailand, where this deliciously rich ice cream originates.

INGREDIENTS
15-ounce can mango,
sliced and drained
¼ cup sugar
juice of 1 lime
1 tablespoon powdered gelatin
1½ cups heavy cream, lightly whipped
fresh mint sprigs, to decorate

SERVES 4–6

COOK'S TIP
Other fruits can be used in this recipe to make flavorful ice creams. If you are looking for a dessert to serve after a spicy main course, choose sharp, tangy citrus fruits such as orange, lemon or grapefruit, which will cleanse and refresh the palate and aid digestion.

1 Reserve 4–6 slices of mango for decoration and chop the remainder into small cubes. Place in a bowl with the sugar. Add the lime juice to the mixture.

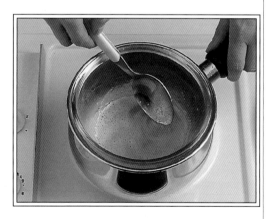

2 Put 3 tablespoons hot water in a small bowl and sprinkle in the gelatin. Place over a pan of gently simmering water and stir until dissolved. Pour onto the cubed mango and mix well.

3 Add the lightly whipped cream and fold into the mango mixture. Pour the mixture into a plastic freezer bag or box and freeze until half frozen.

4 Place in a food processor or blender and blend until smooth. Spoon back into the plastic bag and refreeze.

5 Remove from the freezer 10 minutes before serving and place in the refrigerator. Serve scoops of the ice cream decorated with pieces of the reserved sliced mango, topped with sprigs of fresh mint.

STEWED PUMPKIN IN COCONUT CREAM

tewed fruit is a popular dessert in Thailand. Use the firm-textured Japanese kabocha pumpkin for this dish, if you can. Bananas and melons can also be prepared in this way, or even corn kernels or pulses such as mung beans and black beans, in coconut milk.

INGREDIENTS
2¼ pounds kabocha pumpkin
3 cups coconut milk
6 ounces sugar
pinch of salt
pumpkin seeds, toasted, and
mint sprigs, to decorate

SERVES 4–6

COOK'S TIP
Any pumpkin can be used for this dish, as long as it has a firm texture. Jamaican or New Zealand varieties both make good alternatives to kabocha pumpkin.

1 Wash the pumpkin skin and cut off most of it. Scoop out the seeds.

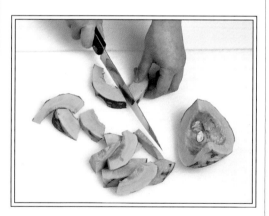

2 Using a sharp knife, cut the flesh into pieces about 2 inches in length and ¾ inch in thickness.

3 In a saucepan, bring the coconut milk, sugar and salt to a boil.

4 Add the pumpkin and simmer for 10–15 minutes, until the pumpkin is tender. Serve warm. Decorate each serving with a few toasted pumpkin seeds and a mint sprig.

COCONUT CUSTARD

This traditional dish from Thailand can be baked or steamed and is often served with a selection of fruit, such as mangoes or tamarillos.

INGREDIENTS
4 eggs
½ cup light brown sugar
1 cup coconut milk
1 teaspoon vanilla, rose or jasmine extract
mint leaves and confectioners' sugar, to decorate
fruit slices, to serve

SERVES 4–6

1 Preheat the oven to 300°F. Whisk the eggs and sugar in a bowl until smooth. Add the coconut milk and the extract and blend well together.

2 Strain the mixture and pour into individual ramekins.

3 Stand the ramekins in a roasting pan. Carefully fill the roasting pan with hot water to reach halfway up the outside of the ramekins.

COOK'S TIP
To test whether custards are set, insert a fine skewer or toothpick into the center of the ramekin. If it comes out clean, they are properly cooked and ready to remove from the oven.

4 Bake for 35–40 minutes or until the custards are set. (See Cook's Tip.)

5 Remove from the oven and let cool. Turn out onto a plate, and serve with sliced fruit. Decorate with mint leaves and a sprinkling of confectioners' sugar.

TAPIOCA PUDDING

This pudding, made from large, pearl tapioca and coconut milk and served warm, is much lighter than the western-style version. You can adjust the sweetness to your taste. Serve with lychees or the smaller, similar-tasting logans—also known as "dragon's eyes."

INGREDIENTS
4 ounces tapioca
2 cups water
6 ounces sugar
pinch of salt
1 cup coconut milk
9 ounces prepared tropical fruits
finely shredded zest of 1 lime,
to decorate

SERVES 4

1 Soak the tapioca in warm water for 1 hour so the grains swell. Drain.

2 Put the water in a saucepan and bring to a boil. Stir in the sugar and salt.

3 Add the tapioca and coconut milk and simmer for about 10 minutes.

4 Serve warm with tropical fruits and decorate with strips of lime zest.

MANGO WITH STICKY RICE

E veryone's favorite dessert. Mangoes, with their delicate fragrance, sweet-and-sour flavor and velvety flesh, blend especially well with coconut glutinous rice. You need to start preparing this dish the day before.

INGREDIENTS
4 ounces white glutinous (sticky) rice
¾ cup thick coconut milk
3 tablespoons sugar
pinch of salt
2 ripe mangoes
strips of lime zest, to decorate

SERVES 4

1 Rinse the glutinous rice thoroughly in several changes of cold water, until the water is clear, then let soak overnight in a bowl of fresh, cold water.

2 Drain the rice and spread in an even layer in a steamer lined with some cheesecloth. Cover and steam for about 20 minutes or until the grains of rice are tender and succulent.

3 Meanwhile, reserve 3 tablespoons of the top of the coconut milk and combine the rest with the sugar and salt in a saucepan. Bring to a boil, stirring until the sugar dissolves, then pour into a bowl and let cool a little.

4 Turn the rice into a bowl and pour in the coconut mixture. Stir, then set aside for 10–15 minutes.

5 Peel the mangoes and cut the flesh into slices. Place on top of the rice and drizzle on the reserved coconut milk. Decorate with strips of lime zest.

FRIED BANANAS

These delicious treats are a favorite with children and adults alike. They are sold as snacks throughout the day and night at portable roadside stalls in Thailand. Other fruits, such as pineapples and apples, work just as well.

INGREDIENTS
4 ounces all-purpose flour
½ teaspoon baking soda
pinch of salt
2 tablespoons sugar
1 egg
6 tablespoons water
2 tablespoons shredded coconut,
or 1 tablespoon sesame seeds
4 firm bananas
oil, for deep-frying
lychees and sprigs of mint, to decorate
2 tablespoons honey, to serve (optional)

SERVES 4

1 Sift the flour, baking of soda and salt into a bowl. Stir in the sugar. Whisk in the egg and add enough water to make quite a thin batter.

2 Whisk in the shredded coconut or sesame seeds.

3 Peel the bananas. Carefully cut each one in half lengthwise, and then crosswise.

4 Heat the oil in a wok or deep-frying pan. Dip the bananas in the batter, then deep-fry in batches in the oil until golden.

5 Remove from the oil and drain on paper towels. Decorate with lychees and sprigs of mint, and serve immediately with honey, if using.

CHINESE-STYLE TOFFEE APPLES

A wide variety of other fruits, such as bananas and pineapples, can be cooked in this way. Sprinkle with sesame seeds for extra crunch.

INGREDIENTS
4 firm apples, peeled and cored
1 cup all-purpose flour
½ cup cold water
1 egg, beaten
vegetable oil, for deep-frying, plus
2 tablespoons for the toffee
½ cup sugar

SERVES 4

1 Cut each apple into 8 pieces. Dust each piece with a little of the flour.

2 Sift the remaining flour into a mixing bowl, then slowly add the cold water and stir to make a smooth batter. Add the beaten egg and blend well.

3 Heat the oil in a wok. Dip the apple pieces in the batter and deep-fry in batches for about 3 minutes or until golden *(left)*. Remove and drain. Heat 2 tablespoons of the oil in the wok, add the sugar and stir constantly until the sugar has caramelized. Quickly add the apple pieces and blend well so that each piece of apple is coated with the "toffee." Dip the apple pieces into cold water to harden before serving.

LIME AND LYCHEE SALAD

T his mixture of fruits in a tangy lime and lychee syrup, topped with a light sprinkling of toasted sesame seeds, makes a refreshing finish to a summer meal.

INGREDIENTS
½ cup sugar
thinly pared zest and juice of 1 lime
14-ounce can lychees in syrup
1 ripe mango, pitted and sliced
1 apple, cored and sliced
2 bananas, chopped
1 star fruit, sliced (optional)
1 teaspoon sesame seeds, toasted

SERVES 4

1 Place the sugar in a saucepan with 1¼ cups water and the lime zest. Heat gently until the sugar dissolves, then increase the heat and boil gently for 7–8 minutes. Remove from heat and let cool.

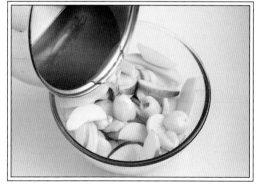

2 Drain the lychee juice into the lime syrup with the lime juice.

3 Place the lychees, mango, apple, bananas and star fruit, if using, in a large bowl and pour in the lime and lychee syrup (left). Cover and chill for 1 hour. Remove from the refrigerator and ladle the fruit salad into a chilled serving bowl. Sprinkle with the toasted sesame seeds and serve.

PINEAPPLE BOATS

A variety of exotic fruits can be used for this fruit salad, depending on what is available. Look for mandarin oranges, star fruit, papaya, Cape gooseberries and passion fruit.

INGREDIENTS
6 tablespoons sugar
1¼ cups water
2 tablespoons crystallized ginger syrup
2 pieces star anise
1-inch piece cinnamon stick
1 clove
juice of ½ lemon
2 mint sprigs
1 mango
2 bananas, sliced
8 lychees, fresh or canned
8 ounces fresh strawberries, trimmed and halved
2 pieces crystallized ginger, cut into sticks
1 pineapple

SERVES 4–6

1 Put the sugar, water, ginger syrup, star anise, cinnamon, clove, lemon juice and mint in a saucepan. Bring to a boil and simmer for 3 minutes. Strain into a large bowl and let cool.

2 Slice off both the top and bottom from the mango and peel off the outer skin. Stand the mango on one end and remove the flesh in two pieces on either side of the large flat pit. Slice the flesh evenly and add to the cooled syrup. Add the bananas, lychees, strawberries and ginger to the syrup. Cover and chill until ready to serve.

3 Cut the pineapple in half lengthwise. Cut out the flesh to make two boat shapes. Cut the flesh into large chunks and place in the cooled syrup.

4 Spoon the fruit into the pineapple halves and serve. There will be enough fruit left over to refill the pineapple halves.

AVOCADO AND LIME ICE CREAM

In China, as in other parts of the world, avocados are frequently eaten as desserts. Their rich texture makes them perfect for a smooth, creamy and delicious ice cream.

INGREDIENTS
4 egg yolks
1¼ cups whipping cream
½ cup sugar
2 ripe avocados
grated zest of 2 limes
juice of 1 lime
2 egg whites
fresh mint sprigs and avocado slices,
to decorate

SERVES 4–6

COOK'S TIP
Ice creams should be quite sweet before they are frozen since they lose some of their flavor when ice cold. Do not store ice cream for too long or ice crystals will form, which will spoil the texture.

1 Beat the egg yolks in a heatproof bowl. In a saucepan, heat the cream with the sugar, stirring it well until the sugar dissolves. As the cream rises to the top of the saucepan at the point of boiling, remove the pan from heat.

2 Gently pour the beaten egg yolks into the scalded cream, adding them in small amounts from a height above the saucepan. This stops the mixture from curdling. Let the mixture cool, stirring occasionally, then chill.

3 Peel and mash the avocados until they are smooth, then beat them into the chilled custard with the lime zest and juice. Check for sweetness.

4 Pour the mixture into a shallow container and freeze until slushy. Beat it well once or twice as it freezes to stop large ice crystals from forming.

5 Whisk the egg whites until softly peaking and fold into the mixture. Freeze until firm. Serve, decorated with mint and avocado.

RED BEAN PASTE PANCAKES

I f you can't find red bean paste, sweetened chestnut purée or mashed dates make good substitutes. Thin pancakes can be bought at Chinese supermarkets and frozen, or you can make your own.

INGREDIENTS
½ cup sweetened red bean paste
8 thin pancakes
2–3 tablespoons vegetable oil
sugar, to serve

SERVES 4

COOK'S TIP
Cooked pancakes can be stored in the freezer. To reheat, warm in a steamer or in a microwave.

1 Spread about 1 tablespoon of the red bean paste on about three-quarters of each pancake, then roll each pancake over three or four times.

2 Heat the oil in a wok or frying pan and shallow-fry the pancake rolls until golden brown, turning once.

3 Cut each pancake roll into 3–4 pieces and sprinkle with sugar to serve.

THIN PANCAKES
To make 24–30 pancakes, sift 4 cups all-purpose flour into a bowl. Slowly stir in 1¼ cups boiling water. Add 1 teaspoon vegetable oil and mix into a firm dough. Cover with a damp cloth and let stand for 30 minutes. Lightly knead the dough on a floured surface for 5–8 minutes until smooth. Divide into thirds. Roll each piece into a cylinder, then cut into 8–10 pieces and roll into balls. Press flat, then roll into 6-inch circles. Heat a small, dry pan and cook one at a time until brown spots appear on the undersides. Stack the pancakes under a damp cloth until you have cooked all of them.

ALMOND CURD JUNKET

Also known as Almond Float, this dessert is usually thickened with agar-agar or isinglass, though gelatin can also be used. It comes from eastern China.

INGREDIENTS
¼ ounce agar-agar or isinglass or
1 ounce gelatin powder
2½ cups water
¼ cup sugar
1¼ cups milk
1 teaspoon almond extract
fresh or canned mixed fruit salad with
syrup, to serve

SERVES 4–6

1 In a saucepan, slowly dissolve the agar-agar or isinglass in half the water over low heat. If using gelatin, follow the manufacturer's instructions.

2 In a separate saucepan, dissolve the sugar in the remaining water over medium heat. Add the milk and the almond extract, blending well, but do not boil.

3 Mix the milk and sugar with the agar-agar or isinglass mixture in a large serving bowl. When cool, place in the refrigerator for 2–3 hours to set.

4 To serve, cut the junket into small cubes and spoon into a serving dish or into individual bowls. Then pour the fruit salad, with the syrup, onto the junket.

GREEN TEA CAKE

Baking cakes for desserts takes on a new twist when using Japanese ingredients. For example, candied adzuki beans *(ama-natto)* are used in the same way as marrons glacés, and the cake remains moist and light.

INGREDIENTS
1 cup all-purpose flour
¹/₂ ounce green tea powder
¹/₂ teaspoon baking powder
3 eggs
¹/₃ cup sugar
¹/₃ cup ama-natto (candied Japanese adzuki beans)
5 tablespoons lightly salted butter, melted
whipped cream, to serve (optional)

MAKES A 7 x 3 x 4-INCH CAKE

1 Preheat the oven to 350°F. Line and grease a loaf pan. Sift the flour, green tea powder and baking powder together and set aside.

2 In a large heatproof bowl, whisk the eggs and sugar over a saucepan of hot water until pale and thick.

3 Sprinkle the sifted flour onto the mixture. Before the flour sinks into the mixture, add the candied Japanese adzuki beans, then fold in the ingredients gently using a spatula. Fold the mixture over from the bottom once or twice. Do not mix too hard. Fold in the melted butter.

4 Pour the mixture into the prepared pan and smooth the top. Bake the cake in the lower part of the oven for 35–40 minutes or until a warm metal skewer inserted into the center of the cake comes out clean.

5 Turn out the cake onto a wire rack and remove the lining paper while it is hot. Let cool. Slice and serve with whipped cream, if desired.

RICE CAKES WITH STRAWBERRIES

Whereas traditionally an ingredient such as adzuki bean paste would have been the sole accompaniment for these rice cakes, in this fairly modern dessert, fresh fruit is also served.

INGREDIENTS
scant ¹/₂ cup shiratama-ko powder
(rice flour)
1 tablespoon sugar
cornstarch, for dusting
10 strawberries
scant ¹/₂ cup canned neri-an *(Japanese soft*
adzuki bean paste), cut into 5 pieces

MAKES 5

1 In a microwave-proof bowl, mix the shiratama-ko powder and sugar. Gradually add a scant 1 cup water. Knead well to make a thick paste.

2 Cover and cook in a microwave for 1¹/₂ –2 minutes. Alternatively, steam in a heatproof bowl over a pan of simmering water for 10–15 minutes.

3 Lightly dust a cutting board with a layer of cornstarch. Turn out the heated mixture onto it and divide it into five even-size pieces. Using a rolling pin, gently roll out a portion of the mixture into a small oval shape.

4 Put a strawberry and a piece of *neri-an* in the middle. Fold the rice cake in half and serve decorated with a strawberry. Make another four rice cakes. Eat the rice cakes on the day they are prepared—if left for any longer, they will harden.

SWEET POTATO, APPLE AND BEAN PASTE CAKES

A mixture of mashed sweet potato and a hint of apple is shaped into cubes, covered in batter and then seared in a hot pan to seal in the natural moisture. Adzuki bean paste is also made into cakes by the same method.

INGREDIENTS
9 ounces canned neri-an *(Japanese soft adzuki bean paste), divided into 3 pieces*

FOR THE BATTER
6 tablespoons all-purpose flour
pinch of sugar
5 tablespoons water

FOR THE STUFFING
5 ounces sweet potato, peeled
¹/₄ apple, cored and peeled
scant 1 cup water
¹/₄ cup sugar
juice of ¹/₄ lemon

SERVES 3 (MAKES 6)

1 Put all the ingredients for the batter in a bowl and mix well until smooth. Pour the batter into a large, shallow dish.

2 Dice the sweet potato and soak it in plenty of cold water for 5 minutes to remove any bitterness, then drain well.

3 Coarsely chop the apple and place in a saucepan. Add the water and sweet potato. Sprinkle in 1¹/₂ teaspoons sugar and cook over medium heat until the apple and potato are softened.

4 Add the lemon juice and remove the saucepan from heat. Then drain the sweet potato and apple and crush them into a coarse paste in a mixing bowl with the remaining sugar.

5 Using your hands, shape the mixture into three cubes.

6 Heat a nonstick frying pan. Carefully coat a cube of stuffing mixture in batter, then, taking great care not to burn your fingers, sear each side of the cube on the hot frying pan until the batter has set and cooked through.

7 Repeat this procedure with the remaining stuffing mixture and with the *neri-an*, shaped into similar-size cubes. Arrange on small plates and serve hot or cold.

239

GREEN AND YELLOW LAYERED CAKES

This colorful two-tone dessert is made by squeezing contrasting mixtures in a small pouch of muslin or thin cotton. The Japanese title, *Chakin-shibori,* is derived from the preparation techniques, in which *chakin* means a pouch shape and *shibori* means a molding action.

INGREDIENTS
FOR THE YOLK MIXTURE (*KIMI-AN*)
6 large eggs
¼ cup sugar

FOR THE PEA MIXTURE (*ENDO-AN*)
1³⁄₄ cups fresh peas, shelled
8 teaspoons sugar

MAKES 6

1 To make the yolk mixture, hard-boil the eggs. Remove the yolks and sieve them into a bowl. Press the yolk with a spatula, add the sugar and mix well.

2 To make the pea mixture, boil the peas for about 15 minutes or until they are softened. Drain and place in a mortar, then crush the peas with a pestle and transfer them to a saucepan.

3 Add the sugar and cook, stirring continuously, until the paste is thick. Keep the mixture simmering, but ensure that it does not stick to the bottom of the pan.

4 Spread out the paste in a large dish to cool it quickly. To maintain its green color, it is important to cool the paste as quickly as possible.

5 Divide each of the mixtures into six portions. Wet a piece of muslin or thin cotton and wring it out well.

6 Place a lump of pea mixture on the cloth and put a lump of the yolk mixture on top. Wrap it up and squeeze the top of the cloth to mark a spiral pattern on the top of the cakes. Squeezing the cloth also binds the two stuffings together. Make another five cakes in the same way. Serve cold.

ACCOMPANIMENTS

In addition to well-spiced dishes, much of Asian cooking also features dipping sauces, pickles and other condiments on the table during a meal. Each cook puts a slightly different slant on a popular recipe, so feel free to adapt them to your taste. Hoisin Dip is basically a barbecue sauce and accompanies spring rolls and prawn crackers. Sambal Goreng and Thai Dipping Sauce are both strong and fiery. Indian breads are definitely worth learning to make if you have the time as the authentic flavors complement spicy dishes perfectly.

PARATHAS

Parathas are a richer, softer and flakier variation of chapatis, but they require a longer preparation time, so plan your menu well in advance.

INGREDIENTS
3 cups atta *(whole-wheat flour), plus
extra for dusting
½ cup all-purpose flour
½ teaspoon salt
2 tablespoons ghee
water, to mix
2 teaspoons ghee, melted*

MAKES 12–15

1 Sift the flours and salt into a mixing bowl. Make a well in the center and add the ghee. Rub in untill the mixture resembles bread crumbs. Slowly add enough water to make a soft but pliable dough. Cover and let stand for an hour.

2 Divide the dough into 12–15 portions and cover. Roll out each into a 4-inch round. Brush each round with a little of the melted ghee and dust with *atta*. Make a straight cut from the center to the edge. Lift a cut edge and form the dough into a cone.

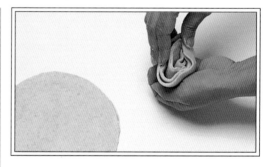

3 Flatten the cone into a ball, then roll out the dough into a 7-inch round. Heat a griddle and cook the parathas one at a time, brushing around the edges with the remaining ghee, until golden brown on each side. Serve hot.

NAAN

Traditionally, this flat leavened bread from northern India is baked in a tandoor or clay oven, although grilled naans look just as authentic.

INGREDIENTS

4 cups all-purpose flour
1 teaspoon baking powder
½ teaspoon salt
2 teaspoons sugar
2 teaspoons active dry yeast
scant 1 cup lukewarm milk
⅔ cup plain yogurt, beaten
1 egg, beaten
¼ cup melted ghee
all-purpose flour, for dusting
chopped cilantro and onion seeds, to sprinkle
ghee, for greasing
edible silver sheets, to serve (optional)

MAKES 6–8

1 Sift the flour, baking powder and salt into a large bowl. Stir in the sugar and yeast. Make a well in the center and add the milk, yogurt, egg and melted ghee. Gradually incorporate the flour mixture to make a pliable dough.

2 Knead the dough for about 10 minutes. Place in a bowl, cover tightly and keep in a warm place until the dough doubles in size. To test, push a finger into the dough—it should spring back. On a floured surface roll out the dough to a ¾-cup thickness.

3 Preheat the oven to 400°F. Roll out 6–8 slipper-shaped naans, about 10 × 6-inch tapering to about 2 inches. Sprinkle with the cilantro and onion seeds. Bake on greased sheets for 10–15 minutes. Serve hot, with silver, if using.

HOT LIME PICKLE

Agood lime pickle is delicious served with any meal. In India, where it originated, it is thought to increase the appetite and help digestion. It takes a long time to prepare, but is worth the wait!

INGREDIENTS
25 limes
1 cup salt
¼ cup fenugreek powder
¼ cup mustard powder
½ cup chili powder
½ ounce turmeric
2½ cups mustard oil
1 teaspoon asafoetida
1 ounce yellow mustard seeds, crushed

MAKES 2 CUPS

1 Cut each lime into 8 pieces and remove the seeds. Place the limes in a large sterilized jar or glass bowl. Add the salt and toss with the limes. Cover and set in a warm place until they become soft and brown in color, for 1–2 weeks.

2 Combine the fenugreek powder, mustard powder, chili powder and turmeric and add to the limes. Cover with a clean cloth and let rest in a warm place for another 2–3 days.

3 Heat the mustard oil in a frying pan and fry the asafoetida and mustard seeds. When the oil reaches the smoking point, pour onto the limes. Mix well, cover and set in a warm place for 1 week before serving.

VIETNAMESE DIPPING SAUCE

 erve this dip in a small bowl as an accompaniment to spring rolls or meat dishes.

INGREDIENTS
1–2 small red chiles, seeded and finely chopped
1 garlic clove, crushed
1 tablespoon roasted peanuts
¼ cup ccoconut milk
2 tablespoons fish sauce
juice of 1 lime
2 teaspoons sugar
1 tablespoon chopped cilantro leaves

SERVES 4

MAKES ²/₃ CUP

1 Crush the red chile together with the garlic and peanuts using a mortar and pestle or food processor. Transfer the mixture to a small bowl.

2 Add the coconut milk, fish sauce, lime juice, sugar and cilantro and serve.

HOT TOMATO SAMBAL

Sambals are placed on the table as a condiment and are used mainly for dipping meat and fish. They are quite strong and should be used sparingly.

INGREDIENTS
3 ripe tomatoes
½ teaspoon salt
1 teaspoon chili sauce
¼ cup fish sauce or soy sauce
1 tablespoon chopped cilantro leaves

MAKES ½ CUP

1 Cover the tomatoes with boiling water to loosen the skins. Remove the skins, halve, discard the seeds and chop finely.

2 Place the tomatoes in a bowl, add the salt, chili sauce and fish sauce or soy sauce. Sprinkle with cilantro and serve.

COOK'S TIP
Hot Tomato Sambal is often used instead of fresh red chiles in many sauces or curries. It can be stored in the refrigerator for up to a week.

SAMBAL GORENG

his sambal makes an excellent, if fiery, side dip for vegetable, fish or meat dishes.

INGREDIENTS
1-inch cube terasi
2 onions, quartered
2 garlic cloves, crushed
1-inch piece lengkuas, *peeled and sliced*
2 teaspoons chili sambal paste or
2 fresh red chiles, seeded and sliced
2 tablespoons oil
3 tablespoons tomato paste
2½ cups stock or water
12 ounces cooked chicken pieces
⅓ cup cooked green beans
¼ cup tamarind juice
pinch of sugar
3 tablespoons coconut milk
salt and freshly ground black pepper

MAKES 3¾ CUPS

COOK'S TIP
For Shrimp Sambal Goreng, add 12 ounces cooked shrimp and 1 green bell pepper, seeded and chopped. For an egg version, add 3 hard-boiled eggs, shelled and chopped, and 2 tomatoes, skinned, seeded and chopped.

1 Process the *terasi* with the onions and garlic into a paste in a food processor or with a mortar and pestle. Add the *lengkuas*, chili sambal paste or sliced chiles and salt. Process or pound into a fine paste.

2 Fry the paste in hot oil for 1–2 minutes, without browning, until the mixture gives off a rich aroma.

3 Add the tomato paste and the stock or water and cook over medium heat for 10 minutes. Add the chicken and beans (or see Cook's Tip for alternatives) and cook for 3–4 minutes. Stir in the tamarind juice, sugar and coconut milk at the last minute. Season with salt and freshly ground black pepper and serve immediately in small dipping bowls.

THAI DIPPING SAUCE

am Prik is the most common dipping sauce in Thailand. It has a fiery strength, so use with caution.

INGREDIENTS
1 tablespoon vegetable oil
1 piece shrimp paste, ½-inch square, or
1 tablespoon fish sauce
2 cloves garlic, finely sliced
1 piece fresh ginger root, ¾ inch long,
peeled and finely chopped
3 small red chiles, seeded and chopped
1 tablespoon finely chopped
cilantro root or stem
4 teaspoons sugar
3 tablespoons dark soy sauce
juice of ½ lime

MAKES ½ CUP

COOK'S TIP
Nam Prik sauce will keep in a screw-top jar for up to 10 days or up to 2 weeks if stored in the refrigerator. As it is such a versatile sauce, suited to many Asian dishes, it's a good idea to make a large amount as it can be frozen for up to 2 months.

1 Heat the vegetable oil in a wok, add the shrimp paste or fish sauce, garlic, ginger and chiles and soften without coloring, for 1–2 minutes.

2 Remove from heat and add the cilantro, sugar, soy sauce and lime juice. Serve in a small bowl.

HOISIN DIP

T his speedy dip needs no cooking and can be made in just a few minutes—it tastes great with spring rolls or shrimp crackers.

INGREDIENTS
4 scallions
1½-inch piece ginger root
2 red chiles
2 garlic cloves
¼ cup hoisin sauce
½ cup passata
1 teaspoon sesame oil (optional)

SERVES 4

COOK'S TIP
Hoisin sauce makes an excellent base for full-flavor dips, especially when combining vegetables and other Asian seasonings.

1 Cut off and discard the green ends of the scallions. Slice the remainder very thinly. Peel the ginger with a swivel-bladed vegetable peeler, then chop it finely.

2 Halve the chiles lengthwise and remove their seeds. Finely slice the flesh crosswise into tiny strips. Finely chop the garlic. Stir together the hoisin sauce, passata, scallions, ginger, chile, garlic and sesame oil, if using, and serve within 1 hour.

INDEX